D1499746

WITHDRAWN

ECONOMIC DYNAMICS

ECONOMIC DYNAMICS

Roy Harrod

MACMILLAN
ST. MARTIN'S PRESS

First published 1973 by
THE MACMILLAN PRESS LTD
London and Basingstoke
Associated companies in New York Toronto
Dublin Melbourne Johannesburg and Madras

Library of Congress catalog card no. 72–88004

SBN 333 14247 0

Printed in Great Britain by
WESTERN PRINTING SERVICES LTD
Bristol

Contents

Preface

Almost immediately after the end of the last World War I received an invitation to give five lectures in the University of London. They were delivered in February 1947 and published in January 1948, under the title of *Towards a Dynamic Economics*. Since that time I have published a number of articles on this theme, which express further developments of my thinking.

Some time ago it occurred to me that on the occasion of the next reprint I ought to make some amendments and additions to the original text.

But when I sat down to this task I found it was no good. It would be needful to rewrite the book completely. I have only retained a few pages here and there from my old text.

I thought I might cast aside the modesty implied in the words 'Towards a . . .'. None the less, I hope that readers will understand that we are still only on the threshold of the subject. This book should be regarded as a first beginning.

It is important that it should be recognised that during the last hundred years economic thinkers have been completing and perfecting the principles of economic statics; this includes the great Keynes himself, who furnished fundamental new ideas. To find any exposition of dynamic principles one has to go back to Adam Smith and Ricardo and their followers. This is a great gap in all modern economics.

I must express my gratitude to Professor Robin Matthews, who was good enough to read my text and make a number of suggestions.

September 1972   R. F. H.

1 The Need for a Dynamic Economics

It seems appropriate to take over from mechanics the dichotomy of statics and dynamics. The word statics has already been familiarly used with reference to one part of economics; dynamics less so.[1] It is often used in a way that does not correspond to the dichotomy of mechanics.

Both parts should have their basic axioms, which should serve as the foundation of empirical research. The basic axioms of statics have long been well established. We may think of them as 'the laws of supply and demand' in the widest sense. But to date, dynamics has been gravely lacking in basic axioms. This remains a handicap.

One would suppose that the kind of empirical study required for building an edifice on the axioms would, in the case of statics, be fieldwork, and in that of dynamics, econometric work. This is only a rough and approximate allocation and must not be pushed too far. Doubtless in both branches there will be scope both for fieldwork and for econometric work, and indeed for the two working together.

In recent years, the expression 'growth economics' has been coming much into vogue. I suggest that this expression has a wider connotation than dynamic economics. Growth economics may appropriately be used for a range of study in which sociological principles play an important part. Indeed it is essential that they should. There is at present a school of thought, with which I strongly sympathise, that urges that academic economists have laid too much stress on the multiplication of material goods. This tendency may even be strengthened by the development of statistical methods for measuring the growth of G.N.P. and by league tables listing the various countries. It is important

---

[1] Cf. John Stuart Mill, *Principles of Political Economy*, Book IV, ch. 1, for both 'statics' and 'dynamics'.

that in this field there should be economists at work, who understand not only the basic economic axioms in the narrow sense, but are also well qualified to handle wider sociological considerations. In dealing with economic growth, one should be thinking in terms of a greater range of human happiness than can be specified by the statistical measurement of the quantum of goods and services. Elements of welfare that lie outside the G.N.P., as commonly specified, may yet belong to economics in the wider sense, as requiring the allocation to them of part of the totality of productive resources available. But, when the inputs of resources have been made, the outputs may not be capable of being the objects of exchange or of being alternatively allocable to different persons, as in the case of the layout of cities or the preservation of the countryside. But, given that, there is some danger that these wider interests may deflect attention from the fact that dynamic economics in the narrow sense urgently needs its set of basic axioms, in which, so far, it has been rather lacking.

There is another dichotomy, much in vogue, that may serve to confuse thinking. In many universities there is a course of study labelled macro-economics. This is contrasted with micro-economics. This is a different division, because part of macro-economics belongs to the field of economic statics and only part to the field of economic dynamics. Both statics and dynamics may be divided into micro-economics and macro-economics. The contribution of Keynes that is now the part of his work that is most studied lies in the field of macro-economics. But it is for the most part, at least in its strictly theoretical part, confined to · the field of statics.

There is yet another dichotomy that is much used by economic writers, that contrasts neo-classical with Keynesian economics. This makes no sense, since in the field of macro-statics, Keynes's great domain, the neo-classical school has hardly anything to contribute. It is not a question here of belonging to one school of thought or another. The two disciplines deal with different domains. There appears to have been some change in the use of the word 'neo-classical' in the last few decades. When I was young, the expression 'classical economics' related to the thoughts of economists from Adam Smith to John Stuart Mill and his contemporaries, while neo-classical related to the more complete system which resulted from the formulation of the idea of marginal utility by Jevons and Karl Menger and the interweaving of that concept throughout the range of economic principles. The term neo-classical has, it seems, more recently been applied to a later phase of economic thinking. The distinctive contribution of these later neo-classicals has not been so clearly specified.

Statics is essentially concerned with a state of rest. Given the whole range of available productive resources, given the state of technology, and given the desires and tastes of the individuals in an economy, how will the resources be divided among alternative uses, what prices will be established for them and what prices for the goods and services produced by them? It is postulated that the market will establish equilibria. In certain cases there may be more than one possible eqilibrium consistent with the data aforementioned. The desire by each person for a given commodity cannot be represented by a single number, but must be represented by a schedule showing the different strengths of desire for the different possible amounts of the commodity. Similarly the productivity of the resources must be represented by schedules. If there are inflections in these schedules, this may lead to alternative possible equilibria.

'State of rest' may give too narrow a definition of the matters covered by micro-statics. It is expedient to include within this discipline possible changes in tastes, availability of resources, etc., provided that these are *once-over* changes. Owing to the interdependence of the whole system of prices and quantities, as set out in simultaneous equations, a single change in one item might conceivably entail changes in all the prices and quantities throughout the field. Before the change one will have determined all prices and amounts produced, by means of the equations specifying the state of affairs at that time. Then, after the change, one will need to do all one's sums again, to determine the amounts of the whole range of outputs and the spectrum of prices, taking into account the effects of the change.

One will be interested, not only in the new state of affairs, but also in the process by which the economy adjusts itself from the old state to the new state. What are the forces at work? It has been suggested that this study of the mode by which the economy moves from one static equilibrium to another should be regarded as part of dynamics. This would be to confuse the issue. We can even now dimly discern the basic axioms of dynamics sufficiently to appreciate that they are not relevant to this study, which should be governed by applying 'the laws of supply and demand' in the widest sense. The realm of dynamics is something quite different. The possibility of cobweb action during a transition and the possibility of multiple equilibria or even ranges of indeterminateness still lie within the domain of micro-statics.

There is yet another dichotomy that has to be considered, namely that between the facts about how an equilibrium is established and the question of whether the state of affairs thus established represents an economic optimum. This connection is illustrated by the reference to one of the great masters of micro-statics in the expression 'Pareto optimum'. It was the tradition of classical economics from Adam Smith onwards to hold that, subject to the operation of frictions, monopolies etc., there was a happy consilience between what was likely actually to happen and what would produce the maximum of social welfare. We must also make a reservation as regards the consequent distribution of income among the various members of the economy. It will eventually be part of the task of dynamic economics to establish the relations between what actually happens and maximum social welfare. It is at this point that, as noted above, sociological considerations must be brought into play.

Prior to the studies of macro-statics (Keynes) there had already been a dent, which may alternatively be judged as great or small, in the harmonious pattern of micro-statics. It may be expedient to have a brief digression here on that topic, since it will be found to have a relation to dynamic economics. In general, traditional micro-statics, especially in its more precise forms, based itself on what may be called an 'atomistic' assumption, namely that each producer was so small a part of the total economy that his own variations of output had no effect on the price of his product. This entailed that, so far as he was concerned, he was confronted by a demand curve of infinite elasticity. A certain contradiction lies hidden here. It was for Mr Piero Sraffa to bring it out into the open in his famous article in the *Economic Journal*.[1] He showed that in this case it

[1] P. Sraffa, 'Laws of Returns under Competitive Conditions' (*Economic Journal*, December 1926).

was impossible for there to be at the equilibrium point a condition of decreasing cost of production. For that condition to obtain there would have to be some measure of monopoly. This was not in accord with what was previously expounded on the blackboard in classes. The lecturer would explain, doubtless with the aid of graphs, that production might be subject at the margin to increasing costs or to decreasing costs. One could expatiate on the conditions in which one or other was likely to obtain. But according to the Sraffa doctrine decreasing costs could not obtain unless the producer had some measure of monopoly and the demand curve confronting him was by consequence downward-sloping.

Mention may be made in passing of a by-product of this doctrine. It had hitherto been assumed that an increase in the demand for a product might cause its price to rise, or, alternatively, at least after immediate bottlenecks were overcome, might cause its price to fall, that depending on whether it was subject to increasing or decreasing costs of production. The new doctrine implied that an increase in demand would normally tend to raise the price. I believe this to be quite wrong. But this idea has suggested that in a time of general price inflation an appropriate way to check it would be to damp down demand all round. This has had a notably unfortunate and perverse effect on policy in the U.K. and the U.S.A., and perhaps elsewhere also, in 1970 and 1971.

In the 1920s I conducted a certain amount of fieldwork and found that the majority of producers claimed that they were in fact subject to decreasing costs and that, if the demand for their products went up, they would be likely to put their prices down. Among these were some who seemed to be in very active competition with other makers of the same article. This result was further confirmed in interviews conducted by the 'Oxford Economists Research Group' in the thirties.

Consideration of these matters led to the development of a scheme of thought known as the 'Theory of Imperfect Competition'. This got away from the classical atomistic doctrine according to which each and every producer could sell as much as he liked at the going national (or world) prices.

Imperfect competition does not imply a monopolistic, or even an oligopolistic position. It was, in my judgement, unfortunate that Professor Chamberlin, whose volume covered the same range of studies, called it 'The Theory of Monopolistic Competition'. Whether a firm should be regarded as monopolistic or oligopolistic depends on its size relatively to the sum total of producers of similar products.

Imperfect competition includes oligopoly and monopoly, but it is not confined to them. It arises whenever a product is not of an absolutely homogeneous character, and this covers most products other than primary products. In this case, the producer can only expand his market by establishing his reputation for quality among a wider range of customers. This takes time and costs effort.

It is sometimes said that, when a product is not absolutely standardised and homogeneous and there are, in consequence, differences in quality or detail between the outputs of a number of producers, each producer ought to be regarded as a 'monopolist' of his own particular product. This is really no more than a verbal quibble and distracts attention from more fundamental matters. For most purposes, when products have what common sense regards as a reasonable degree of similarity and are called by the same name – e.g. writing desks, jumpers, etc. – their producers should be regarded as all producing the same product, even although there are some differences of quality and detail between them. There may be monopoly or oligopoly in such cases; but there need not be. There is, however, imperfect competition, because each producer cannot sell as much as he wants at a given price fixed externally to himself on a national or world market. He is not confronted by a demand curve of infinite elasticity.

With imperfect competition there is a downward-sloping demand curve, even although there may be no monopoly or oligopoly in an acceptable sense of those words. With a downward-sloping demand curve it is possible for there to be equilibrium at a point where there are decreasing costs of production in each and every firm producing the product in question. This also applies to services, which are of growing relative importance in advanced economies.

In each case where there are decreasing costs, a rise in demand may be expected to reduce the price, apart, sometimes but not always, from short-period bottlenecks. Thus, except when an economy is working more or less to full capacity, a general rise in demand should be expected to cause a fall in prices on the overall average.

The last proposition is in conflict with doctrine that has been in vogue in recent years. It has been held that if prices are rising, a sovereign remedy is to reduce overall demand. This has had an unfortunate consequence by distracting attention from wage-price spiralling, which is an entirely different phenomenon, and, if it is to be corrected, will have to be corrected by methods entirely different from that of reducing aggregate effective demand in the economy.

We may now pass to macro-statics, into the domain of which we have already been trespassing. It is in this field that Keynes has been the all-important master. The classical scheme had its main success in the determination of how productive resources are distributed in the production of the different kinds of goods and services, in the pricing of those goods and services and of the factors of production themselves. But it did not have much to contribute about the question of the degree to which productive resources would tend to be utilised. If we ask how an individual will distribute his income among various products, he will argue that the more he buys of each product the less its 'marginal' utility will be to him so that he will push on with the purchase of each until the marginal utilities of each are proportional to the respective prices that have to be paid for them. This is not only correct, as a matter of pure theory, but has also a reasonable degree of application to the realities of life.

By analogy with this, when faced with the question of the degree to which productive resources will be utilised, one might argue that each person will work just so hard as to make the marginal disutility of his work equal to the utility of what that work produces. But here we are departing far from the realities of life in most spheres. The doctrine might apply well enough to some Robinson Crusoe. It may also apply in cases of peasant proprietors, who have full command of their own time and are working in perfect competition, i.e. able to sell as much as they can produce at a given price fixed externally to themselves, which may be deemed to be proportional to the marginal utility of the product in the world economy as a whole. Strictly, such a peasant proprietor must have a rather canny understanding of the money yield of toiling in the field for an extra hour a day. Then he can measure that against the toilsomeness of doing so. There may be certain areas, especially in rather primitive communities, where this principle actually operates, but for most workers the amount of work done depends on different forces. And here classical economics is somewhat barren of ideas.

There are those who are doing no work at all, but would be willing to work at the rate of pay currently offered for such work, namely the 'unemployed'. They might even be willing to work for a slightly lower 'real' wage, namely at the wage currently offered, but with the prices of goods rather higher than they are. Keynes refers to this as 'involuntary' unemployment, to distinguish it from frictional unemployment that occurs during a time interval in which workers have to look for work from an alternative employer or even in an alternative type of production, and again from those who prefer to be idle, living at a lower level from State assistance, even when jobs for which they are qualified are available.

We then have to go over to the employers. What determines the amount of employment that they are willing and able to give? In the field of micro-statics one has to consider of course the rise or fall in the demand for their particular products. But it has for more than a century been evident that there are times when the average of the demands for all products is laggard. This became evident in relation to business cycles. Keynes's theories have relevance for the analysis of business cycles; but they also have a wider relevance. In many generations the kind of analysis of the business cycle undertaken by experts on it was somewhat detached from general economic theory as exemplified in the general theory of values already discussed.

It may be expedient to set out in a few sentences the central core of Keynes's theory of the amount of aggregate demand obtaining at any time, which in its turn would govern the level of employment. It may be noted that this, while in the end presumably the most important, was only one among a vast range of contributions made by Keynes to economics, which may be studied in his collected works, that, at the time of writing, have begun to appear.

Aggregate demand has two main components, the demand for fixed or working capital and the demand for end products to be consumed. Both categories include some demand coming from Governments, central and local. There is also the demand for exports, equally balanced, or not equally balanced, by the supply of imports, a topic on which Keynes did not work extensively in relation to the particular theory of aggregate demand that we are now discussing.

The demand for capital goods will depend on the estimates that their buyers make of their most likely need for such goods in connection with the volume of output of the goods that they are geared to produce, which may of course also be capital goods. In most cases, especially as regards the fixed capital that they require, they will have to look ahead for a substantial period of time. In some cases it may be possible to make precise estimates; in others these may depend on the variable factor of 'expectations', which can have a strongly psychological element. Keynes did much interesting work on the topic of expectations.

If we add together all the estimates made by the various buyers of capital goods, we may find that it would take 15 per cent – let us be bold and start with an arithmetical example – of all the productive resources of the economy, supposing these to be fully employed, to make them. Let us suppose that persons and companies want to save 84 per cent of their net incomes. Net overall income is necessarily equal to the current overall output of the economy. The two percentages that I have mentioned add up to 99 per cent. It will then be the case that the aggregate demand for capital and consumer goods will be less than the economy is capable of producing. If net income receivers wished to spend 90 per cent of their net incomes, aggregate demand would be for something greater than the economy is capable of producing. In the former case the shortfall will be somewhat more than 1 per cent; the 15 per cent is a fraction of what the total output would be with full employment; the 84 per cent relates to actual income. In these conditions the sum of the demand for capital goods and the fraction of their net incomes that persons and companies wish not to save amounts to about 94 per cent[1] of what the economy is capable of producing.

[1] $15 + 84\%$ of $94 = 93 \cdot 96$.

In this case there would be 6 per cent unemployment. The number 'walking the streets' need not be so high, as there may be underemployment inside the factories. But this 'underemployment' has nothing to do with the willingness of workers to work. It is, so to speak, an institutional friction.

It is to be strongly stressed that in this account there is no reference to money. We have referred to a certain quantum of fixed and circulating capital as being a fraction of what the economy is capable of producing, and we have referred to the saving of persons and companies as a fraction of their net incomes. These two fractions are both expressed in real terms.

This has bearings in two directions. By the so-called classical economics an unemployment situation could be remedied by a decline in wages. Some have suggested that the essence of Keynes' doctrine depends on a resistance to downward revisions of wages. Such a resistance is indeed a fact of modern life, but it has nothing to do with the essential Keynesian doctrine. There is no reference in that doctrine to the level of wages, or, indeed to the level of prices.

Nor is there any reference to money, and this has a second bearing. Here we may note yet another often quoted dichotomy! It is that between Keynesians and monetarists. It is to be stressed that Keynes attached the greatest importance to the influence of money and monetary policy, but he did not hold that an increase of the money supply would have any direct influence on prices. The story of how the first of my two percentages is established, namely the producers' assessment of the future, including their expectations, needs to be somewhat modified to comply with Keynesian doctrine. We must not include in that fraction plans for capital extensions that they would be likely to put into operation, but cannot for lack of available funds. An increase in the money supply will create redundant money holdings and thereby make it easier to raise money for capital purposes. This will increase the former of the two fractions. But it may be that no feasible increase in the money supply will increase the former fraction sufficiently to make the two fractions add up to 100 per cent. It has been argued by some monetary theorists that consumers will spend some of their increased money supply. This could be true in exceptional cases but it seems an unlikely event. The money will come into them as a by-product of bank operations and they would normally seek to reinvest it. It is highly unlikely that an increase in the money supply will alter their regular ideas about how to divide their income between saving and spending.

There is a different way in which an increase in the money supply could impinge on consumption, and this is by making consumer credit easier to come by. If an increase in the money supply did not achieve full employment, then, or indeed, perhaps without waiting, we should bring into action Keynes' sovereign remedy, now commonly called 'fiscal policy'. Let the Government run a Budget deficit, i.e. dis-save. This would raise the fraction of national income devoted to consumption. The Government should dis-save enough to make that fraction and the fraction of available productive resources required for capital outlay plans add up to unity. Conversely, if the sum of the two fractions exceeds unity, the Government should run a Budget surplus sufficient to reduce them to unity.

Micro-dynamics should deal with forces governing the rates of increase (or of decrease) of demand for particular commodities, or those governing the rates of increase or decrease in the prospects of particular firms or industries. It enters into the theory of firm decision making, on which valuable work is being done.

Macro-dynamics, with which this book deals, is concerned with the determinants of the rates of increase of the main categories of demand – those for capital goods, for exports, etc. This is where we have a lacuna in Keynes. He has no systematic theory about this matter. Owing to inevitable uncertainties, when we are looking into the future, the sum total of assessments made by firms may be too high or too low. This is quite a different point from the possibility that the sum of the two fractions just quoted may be greater or less than one. Of course, expectations may be influenced upwards or downwards by infections of optimism or pessimism. Keynes has much of great interest to say about the volatility of expectations. But he has no account of the forces that determine what they *ought* to be.

Keynes was wrongly accused by D. H. Robertson and Sir John Hicks of leaving the rate of interest hanging by its own bootstraps. There is in Keynes a 'neutral' rate of interest (which is, incidentally, a static concept), defined as that interest rate, of all interest rates, that is consistent with full employment. If we ask what forces determine the level of the neutral rate, they prove to be, as in classical economics, the propensity to save and the propensity to invest.[1] But it may fairly be said of Keynes that he does leave expectations hanging by their own bootstraps.

I should claim that the old classical economics contains in roughly equal proportions what I define as static and dynamic elements. The dynamic elements have dropped out of what we now regard as the corpus of economic principles. As the static analysis came to be refined and perfected by the use of the marginal concept and by mathematical expression, the dynamic analysis fell out of view. This may have been particularly due to the fact that Dynamics did not give such scope to the marginal analysis. The lapse of Dynamics from favour is most remarkably illustrated by Marshall. We know well how lovingly he treasured all the bits and pieces of traditional theory. He could not bear to abandon the view that the rent of land does not enter into the cost of production. Even the iron law of wages reappears; its guise is softened and rendered kindly, but it is there all the same. To make sure of my ground I re-read Marshall's Principles before composing this, and I can find scarcely any trace of that dynamic theory which occupied at least half of the attention of the old classical school.[2]

We may take as an illustration Ricardo himself. In his preface we can find the famous words 'to determine the laws that regulate this distribution is the principal problem in Political Economy'. A modern reader is grammatically entitled to take these words as referring to what we now know as the static theory of distribution. But we should regard them in the light of the earlier words: 'In different stages of society the proportion of the whole produce of the earth which will be allotted to these classes under the name of rent, profit and wages, will be essentially different.' If one turns back to the preface after reading the book one is certainly driven to interpret the first quoted passage in the light of the other one, that is, to interpret distribution in a dynamic sense, the economist's first task being, not to determine how the product will be apportioned among the

---

[1] I have dealt with this at greater length in *Money*, pp. 175–8.

[2] Perhaps I do less than justice to Marshall; Dynamics might have appeared, after all, in his fourth volume which he never completed.

factors at one time, but how progress successively reapportions the product among the factors.

May I give the bare bones of Ricardo's Dynamic Theory? It was a large part of his whole theory. The prime motive force for him was the tendency to accumulate. This may be identified with what we regard as saving, and is rightly treated by Ricardo as a dynamic concept. He is not guilty of the error, which has crept into textbooks up to the present day of bringing saving into a static system of equations. So long as there is any positive saving, the shape of the economy is progressively altering. This tendency to accumulate has the effect, in accordance with the Wages Fund theory, which Ricardo held in substance, although not in name, of raising the market rate of wages. This, in accordance with Malthusian doctrine, would make the population increase. By the law of diminishing returns, the marginal product of capital and labour would, owing to the population increase, fall through time; but since the population increase would be geared to maintain wages steady at the subsistence – or, as in fairness to Ricardo we may call it, at the equilibrium level – the share of labour in the marginal product would rise, the amount of real wages remaining constant. Consequently the real profit per unit of capital would fall. This is true, whether with Ricardo we use a labour measure of value or an output measure. Rents meanwhile would rise. This is a complete, if crude, dynamic theory. So long as any savings exist, the distribution of wealth continues to change according to certain principles – rents rise, profits fall.

The question was raised – what would happen when profit fell to zero? Long before this, Ricardo replied, the motive for accumulation would have been removed. Thus he contemplated the advent of a stationary state with the rate of interest still positive.

I need hardly stress how important this dynamic theory was in the corpus of doctrine then known as Political Economy. The practical maxim of Free Trade was derivable from static theory. Hardly less important in the minds of contemporaries were those two other practical maxims, (1) that saving by those of means would confer more lasting benefit on the labouring poor than charity, and (2) that the main method open to the poor for self-improvement was to raise their concept of a proper standard of living and by consequence reduce their birth-rate. This of course went with the negative doctrine that it is useless to struggle for higher wages by bargaining or legislation; one could only affect real wages by restricting the supply of labour, which meant holding the population increase in check.

It is difficult to assess the importance in subsequent history of these two practical maxims derived from the old dynamic theory. Historians following Weber have found more ancient and deep-seated causes in Puritanism for the high esteem in which saving was held during the heyday of capitalism. But surely a little may be allowed for the fact that well-educated persons in the nineteenth century, cognisant with political economy, found there the strongest possible endorsement for the view that saving was a virtue. Saving according to this doctrine was not merely a self-regarding virtue, but a humane virtue, tending more than any other form of activity to the betterment of mankind. As regards the second maxim, history has certainly taken the course prescribed by the economists. The labouring poor did in due course begin to restrict their numbers; they could hardly have made the great advances recorded in the last half-century had they not done so. Whether there is any link between the persistent teaching of the economists over several decades and the growth of the birth-control movement is more difficult to determine.

These practical doctrines subsequently passed into disfavour, along with the dynamic theory on which they were based. The dynamic theory was crude, in part untenable as universal law, and in part untenable altogether. But nothing has been put in the place of this theory (or of the maxims); and the corpus of theoretical economics that we teach today right up to and including Keynesian doctrine remain almost exclusively static. The idea that Keynes is more dynamic than Ricardo is the exact opposite of the truth.

Marshall did not live long enough to get his ideas about progress into order and write his projected fourth volume.[1] But John Stuart Mill did incorporate in his 'Principles of Political Economy' a Book 4, entitled 'The Influence of the Progress of Society on Production and Distribution'.[2] The first chapter starts: 'The three preceding parts include as detailed a

[1] See p. 12, footnote 2.   [2] See p. 1, footnote.

view as our limits permit, of what, by a happy generalisation of a mathematical phrase, has been called the Statics of the subject.' And the last two sentences of his first paragraph run 'We have still to consider the economical condition of mankind as liable to change, and indeed (in the more advanced portions of the race, and in all regions to which their influence reaches) as at all times undergoing progressive changes. We have to consider what these changes are, what are their laws, and what their ultimate tendencies; thereby adding a theory of motion to our theory of equilibrium – the Dynamics of political economy to the Statics.' It could hardly be better expressed.

Mill's Book 4 contains some great classic pieces of English literature. There are pleas that the Government should spend plenty of money on public works. Mill here passes out of the traditional classical fear about an insufficiency of saving. There are passages in the Book reminiscent of Professor Kenneth Galbraith. But he does not take the pure theory much beyond what we already have in his predecessors. His anxieties about population increase are very strong.

And then, in due course, in the later part of the century, dynamic economics disappears from view. The cause for this was probably the intellectual excitement generated by theories of marginal utility and marginal productivity, perfected in the edifices of Walras, Pareto and Alfred Marshall. It is only in comparatively recent times that economists have again turned their attention to Dynamics.

2 Fundamental Equations

The most basic equations in dynamics relate to a particular point of time. We may see a train at rest or we may watch it passing a level crossing at a constant velocity. It is then a question of specifying precisely the forces that make it move forward at that velocity. It may also be accelerating or decelerating at that particular point of its journey. Similarly with the rates of increase in an economy.

Dynamic laws do not necessarily involve the presence or analysis of time-lags. I disagreed with Sir John Hicks when, in his early writing, he differentiated dynamic economics as constituting an approach necessarily involving the assignment of dates to particular events. There may, of course, be inflections or discontinuities in rates of increases. In this case, it is necessary to have theories concerning time-lags. But the analysis of forces operating when there is a steady continuous rate of increase (or acceleration, etc.) has logical priority and should be undertaken first. We are then in a good position to proceed to inflections and time-lags.

$$ G = \frac{s}{C} \quad \dots \dots \dots \dots \dots \quad (\text{1}) $$

G is a growth rate per unit of time. We may alternatively write it

$$ \frac{\Delta Y}{Y} $$

where Y stands for income. s is the fraction of income that is saved. C is the accretion of capital in the same unit of time divided by the increment of goods produced in that time.

This equation is a dynamised version of the fact that investment is always necessarily equal to saving.

The correctness of the formula given above cannot be disputed; it is a necessary truth. The only question that can be raised about it is whether it is useful. There is an infinite number of necessary truths. We select those that we hope will be useful tools of thought and may help us to sort out the facts of life in an illuminating way, lead us on to have an understanding of particular facts, and help us to make statements about them that are not always necessary truths. It should be noted that representing saving as a fraction of income does not imply that saving has a functional relation to the size of income, although we may think it reasonable to believe that it does have such a relation.

I now proceed to another equation.

$$G_w = \frac{s_d}{C_r} \quad \ldots \ldots \ldots \ldots \ldots (2)$$

This equation may be regarded, in the first instance at any rate, as a definition of G_w. s_d is the fraction of income that would be represented by the amount of saving that people currently want to make. People are constituted by persons and companies. Is it appropriate to include Government savings? Here a distinction must be drawn, which somewhat anticipates matters. We may think of Governments, central or local, having in mind that it is proper and appropriate for them to make some savings, and we may call those savings what they 'desire' to make. But we should exclude from desired Government savings those that are made to regulate the economy and would not be made if it were not intended to regulate the economy in a certain way. Here we are in the field of what is known as 'fiscal policy'. Governments may also save less than they would otherwise be inclined to, in order to regulate the economy. This 'regulation' is specifically the use of this weapon to influence upwards or downwards the amount of aggregate demand in the economy. What the Government 'desires' to save should be reckoned net of saving or dis-saving done solely to 'regulate' the economy. Once again, it may be noted that, while the amount that people desire to save is represented in the equation as a fraction of their income, it is not implied that what people desire to save is governed by the size of their income, although once again we may well believe that it is, at least partly, so governed.

Persons (and companies) may find that the rate at which their savings are proceeding is deficient or excessive. It is, perhaps, theoretically possible for persons to have no particular views about what they want to be saving. They just let their savings accumulate uncritically as a sort of residual. This might be the condition of very rich people, or, perhaps one should say, it might have been the condition of very rich people in times past. They just enjoy all that they want to in life and never bother to look at their bankbooks and tot up the cost. If there are such, the possible existence of this class of indifferent people does not affect the argument that follows, provided that there are some people who are not so indifferent.

If a man has to overdraw on his bank in order to pay insurance premiums, he will say to himself that it is needful for him to cut down on his consumption and thereby save more than he is doing. The opposite position is also quite possible; a man's income may increase without his immediately adapting his consumption, so that his bank balance builds up. He may then think that he can relax somewhat, and buy some of those extra commodities or services that he has long wished to enjoy. s_d is the rate of saving that he will seek to adhere to, given his income.

C_r is again a fraction. In C without a suffix the numerator is the increase in the volume of goods of all kinds outstanding at the end of the unit period over that outstanding at the beginning of the period, and the denominator is the increment of the production of goods in that period. C becomes C_r when the values of the numerator and denominator are such that people find that the amount of capital goods on hand, fixed and circulating, is just what they find convenient, neither too much nor too little. Expressing capital on hand in this way, carries the suggestion that the quantity of capital desired has a definite relation to the increase in the turnover of goods. That seems reasonable enough in the case of a steady advance. Of course if in the last period there was an excess or deficiency of capital on hand, current capital formation will need to be less or greater than that required for the increment of total output. Once again, it is not necessarily implied that they do judge the sufficiency or insufficiency of capital on hand exclusively by this criterion.

Thus we have a two-fold state of contentment, on the one side by people in regard to what they are currently saving, and on the other side by people in regard to the amount of capital goods, fixed or circulating, that they have on hand.

We then return to our basic equation. We define as G_w that value of G that is consistent with s being equal to s_d and C to C_r. Except in the unlikely event of there being a range of indeterminateness, either for s_d or C_r, there will be a unique value of G, the growth rate of the economy, which is consistent with people saving that they want to save and having the capital goods that they require for their purposes. I have called this value for G the 'warranted' growth rate (G_w).

In my early writing I had hoped that I had thereby established what might be called an equilibrium growth rate, analogous to the traditional equilibrium in a static economy. Doubt was, however, thrown on this by Professor Sidney Alexander in an article in the *Economic Journal*, December 1950, and I have felt bound to acknowledge the justice of his criticism. Equilibrium implies that the various parties to processes are content with what is proceeding and continue to carry on in the same way. But what is carrying on in the same way? I have assumed that if, in the preceding period, they had increased their orders by a certain amount, and if all had gone well, they would decide that, their rate of expansion having turned out all right, they would continue to expand at the same rate. Of course, the different industries and firms will not be expanding at the same rate as each other, they will have their own rates appropriate to their own specifities. Furthermore, some may have made errors, and, indeed, are almost bound to have done so. We say that $C = C_r$ when the aggregate of excesses is equal to the aggregate of deficiencies.

The problem raised by Professor Alexander is how we ought to define 'carrying on in the same way'. Is it possible that the representative placer of orders might argue that, as the orders which he had placed in the last round had turned out all right, he would continue placing orders at that absolute level? The idea that G_w is an equilibrium rate of expansion implies a certain behavioural parameter in the representative entrepreneur. Will he, all having turned out well, continue in his previous growth rate? Or will he stay put at the same absolute level of orders? Or, if he were an optimist, he might decide to speed up his rate of increase. There is the question of the level of what Keynes called the 'animal spirits' of the representative entrepreneur. Recent experience has suggested that at least in the U.K. and the U.S.A., entrepreneurs have been somewhat deficient in animal spirits. If this is more than a chance aberration, it will prove to have a significant bearing on the correct criteria for economic policy.

For the time being we can stand firm on the proposition that the second equation simply gives a definition of what we may call the 'warranted' growth rate. Before proceeding, it will be expedient to present another equation. Can G_w, whether or not it is an equilibrium, be regarded as an optimum? One's mind reverts to classical statics where the equilibrium, apart from monopoly or oligopoly, or, later, imperfect competition, is also an optimum.

The warranted growth rate is in part determined by what people want to save. By analogy with classical statics, in which a certain optimum is achieved by giving freedom to people to buy as much or as little of the various goods as they desire at the equilibrium prices, it could be argued that, as regards saving, which means foregoing present for the sake of future benefit, the social optimum could be achieved by allowing each person freedom to make his own choice between current and future benefit. What the economy as a whole saves will result from the free choices made by all its members. They will be affected by the rate of interest, of which much in due course will be said.

But does this really make sense?

What each person chooses in regard to saving is governed by various institutional arrangements, which differ from country to country and from time to time. There is the question of what the State will provide for future contingencies – old age, ill health, unemployment, etc. – by current transfer payments as and when they arise. The more ground that the State covers, the less will the individual feel it incumbent to provide for himself by saving. Personal saving will also be affected by the degree to which the education of one's children is subvented by the public authorities. Again, when people are thinking of saving for the benefit of their offspring, the whole question of estate duties enters powerfully in. Then the amount of company saving will be much influenced by the facilities provided by the market for new issues of capital. These again differ from country to country. If a company provides a substantial part of its capital disposal by issuing shares, it is using the savings of persons and will thereby not have to save so much by ploughing back profit. In the face of all these complexities and differences of institutional arrangements, both by place and time, it surely cannot be thought that the sum total of what persons and companies want to save for their own convenience can represent any kind of social optimum. If s_d does not represent a social optimum, then by consequence G_w does not either.

Let us symbolise the social optimum rate of growth by G_n. There are two determinants of the value of G_n, the rate of increase of the working population and the rate of improvement in available technology for the production of goods and services. One must not at this point introduce the rate of increase of capital equipment: that would be to put the cart before the horse.

It is needful to refine upon the concept of the increase of working population. The main determinant of this is the number of persons within certain age limits. Men and women may have to be considered separately, whether because social habits cause a larger (or smaller) fraction of women in the various age groups to desire to take jobs, or because previous improvements in infant mortality are causing a shift in the proportions of men and women in the working age groups.

It is naturally assumed that full employment is maintained, subject to inevitable frictional unemployment due to the changing of jobs.

There may be proceeding some reduction in the length of the working life and also in the lengths of the working year, week or day. Optimal arrangements in these respects would presumably normally only be changing if some positive technological progress was being registered. There might of course be some psychological change of attitude due to deep-seated non-economic causes. Usually one would increase one's leisure preference only if there was an increase in goods and services for occupying and enriching leisure time. Thus one would suppose that optimal working time would not be cut back in full proportion to increased output per hour, but less than in proportion.

In some conditions there might be no cut-back at all. This

might well be so in advanced countries. It may probably be said that basically man prefers work to leisure, provided that the work is not so extended as to produce extreme fatigue. In former times do-gooders and representatives of employees gave foremost attention to cutting down work-time. Much more important in advanced conditions is that work in factory or shop should be interesting and a challenge to the creative powers of the employees. Thus a new technological device should be assessed, not only by reference to the increase in output per hour that it makes possible, but also by its effect, if introduced, on the interest and pleasure-giving quality of the work of those who have to implement it. Thought is moving in this direction, but its ambit is not wide-ranging enough. In the past trade unions have often opposed technological improvements on the ground that they would displace workers, who might not find it easy to obtain other jobs. In a country whose authorities were firmly committed, without doubt or question, to maintaining full employment, this anxiety on the part of workers should disappear. Then the unions would be free to concentrate on the question of whether a proposed technological innovation did, or did not, make their working life more dreary. There should in all cases be established machinery for letting them assess whether the increased pay associated with increased output did or did not overweigh the increased dreariness of work, when it caused such. It would be very difficult often, doubtless, to establish means for getting a valid assessment by those concerned. Precisely such difficulties are in the province of sociology, which is hopefully supposed to be going to make progress in the years ahead.

In some cases the elasticity of the demand for goods and services in terms of work may be above one. In such cases higher pay per hour may make those receiving it want to work longer hours. One thinks of Indian villages, where the amount of work done is very low and the reward for work also very low. An increase of returns to each hour worked makes the workers want to work more hours. In such cases an increase of technological facilities would have a double effect in increasing the optimal growth rate; it would increase output per hour and simultaneously increase the optimal number of hours worked.

The optimal length of the working life is clearly influenced by the number of years cut off at its beginning by education at the various levels. Presumably technological progress increases the extra productivity consequent upon an extra year, or whatever it may be, at school or university, taking the overall average of those being equipped by education to participate thereafter in the productive process.

A sceptic may be permitted to pause in doubt for a moment. In the field of services, which is a growing section of total economic activity, it seems that, whereas in former times a query, involving perhaps complex issues, could only be answered by the use of intelligence, it is now answered by pressing a few buttons. And, if the answer to the query provided by button-pressing is challenged by the customer, the button-presser is absolutely flummoxed. An economist has better opportunities for judging in the field of services – shops, banks, etc. – than in what goes on inside factories, except in the case of an economist who has specialised heavily in the study of a particular industry, say steel production, and who thus may have a deep knowledge about what proceeds in the factories concerned. On the face of it, one would suppose that *less* education would be required for performing these press-button functions than for having to use intelligence in dealing with the problems presented. Of course, education cannot alter the amount of intelligence with which each person is endowed. Rather, it serves to enlarge the power of a given intelligence to cope with the problems that will in due course confront it. If that is too idealistic a view of education, then it would be well to hold the amount of time devoted to it down to a minimum. If it is indeed true that technological progress entails, on the overall average, less use of the intelligence, then the optimal plan would be to decrease, on the overall average, the time spent on education.

However, this sceptical note having been sounded, I would assume it sensible to suppose that technological progress raises the optimal time that should be deducted from working life, on the overall average, by education. Thus there is an offset to the growth due to technological progress, owing to its decreasing the optimal length of working life and thereby reducing the increase of the labour force available for production.

In describing the first of the two determinants of the optimal growth rate, it has been assumed that the increase (or decrease) in the number of those of working age is given exogenously; and that the determinants of the optimal number of hours worked per person arise from individual preference curves as between work, goods and leisure.

The former assumption goes violently against classical economics, which held that the rate of population increase was endogenously determined by the rates of reward to labour. The harsher school held that there would be a persistent tendency for the reward of employment to move to the subsistence level. Any higher reward would stimulate an additional increase in the supply of labour. The milder Ricardo held that the main mass of people might be persuaded to limit births, so as to maintain the standard of living above the bare subsistence level. All the same, the rate of increase of population would be endogenously determined.

This population doctrine was linked with stress on the importance of diminishing returns from the land and the tendency to the exhaustion of mines.

In a simplified form the doctrine was as follows. Technological progress in the short run raises rewards to employees; this causes them to have more children; this leads to the need to intensify the exploitation of the land and mines; this increased exploitation involves diminishing returns to the labour engaged on it; these diminishing returns will precisely offset the higher returns due to technical progress.

In modern times this account seems grossly exaggerated and unrealistic. But there are elements in it that should not be overlooked.

First, we may consider diminishing returns. Technological advance impinges directly on farming processes – it has done so most notably in recent years – and on extractive processes. With progress, the area of these diminishing returns sectors tends to decline relatively to the economy as a whole. For simplicity we may define the growth due to technological progress *net*. If the improvements made possible by new technological knowledge were no greater than to offset diminishing returns from the land and the progressive exhaustion of mineral deposits, we could then just write down growth due to technological advance as zero. By this definition *net* technological progress has had a positive value in most parts of the world for a considerable period.

Are we justified in regarding population increase as an exogenous determinant of growth? In this respect the classical economists, who did not so regard it, laid special emphasis on the birth-rate. The idea was that, if per caput income of the main mass of people rose, they would cease refraining from having more children. How did they do this? In those days there were no 'pills'. As a young man, John Stuart Mill was put into prison for flicking over advertisements of more primitive contraceptive devices into area basements in London. Malthus, a clergyman, disapproved of such expedients and held that population should be held down by restraint in the sexual act; but he was entirely sceptical about the likelihood that the main mass of people would in fact exercise such restraint. The logical conclusion of this view is not that the population will always tend to breed up to the subsistence level, but that the birth-rate is an exogenous variable.

What the classical economists appear not to have appreciated was that the vast increase of population in the U.K. that was occurring in their time was due, not to a rising birth-rate, but to a decline in the death-rate, especially in the younger age groups. The birth-rate remained remarkably stable. But this means that the population increase was not an altogether exogenous variable. To the extent that technological progress outstripped diminishing returns, a better diet could be provided, which was good for health. Furthermore, there was rapid medical technological progress, by which the ravages of diseases such as smallpox were greatly reduced.

These considerations may not have great relevance for advanced countries now, subject to what has still to be said, since the area of diminishing-returns products has shrunk and the further decline of deaths due to continuing medical progress is only slight. But they do have great relevance to some less developed countries like India. In them food, which is subject to diminishing returns, is a larger fraction of the total of goods and services consumed. If technological progress, mainly imported, outstrips diminishing returns, this may be expected to reduce the death-rate and thereby increase the rate of population growth. Recently we have had a striking example of technological progress in the form of the 'Green Revolution'. So far this has only affected some parts of India, the different areas of which are largely self-subsistent as regards food; some areas do not grow rice or wheat. Furthermore there is still great scope in a number of less developed countries for an increase of medical technological know-how, mainly imported, and of the associated facilities, to reduce the death-rate and thus cause the rate of population increase to be greater than it otherwise would have been. Thus, to the extent that diminishing returns prevail, there will be an offset to the growth induced by technological progress, home-brewed or imported.

What of the birth-rate? It did not increase when the classical economists were talking so much about it, except in Ireland. But it began to decline strongly in the advanced countries in the middle of the nineteenth century. This was at the same time that the standard of living of the main mass of people began to rise in consequence of the industrial revolution. This seems to violate the central thesis of classical economics, by which a rise in living standards should have stimulated births and not the other way round.

One might frame an opposite hypothesis. When people are living in direst poverty, things cannot be worse, but children are a pleasure in their own right. But when people begin to rise above bare subsistence, they begin to take more note of what money can buy and of how, by using the extra money coming in, they can make their lives more agreeable. And then they may begin to balance this against the pleasure of having yet another child.

We may be in the presence of a U-shaped curve. When the main mass of people become so well off that they can buy most of the material goods that they desire, and when the additional goods that they can buy with rising income do not mean very much to them, then the pleasure to be derived from an extra child may come to the fore again. This may account for the upward tendency in the birth-rate that has manifested itself in some advanced countries since the Second World War.

Bearing in the background of the mind these important interrelations, it may be expedient to begin the study of growth, especially in the moderately short term, by regarding the increase of the working population as an exogenous variable.

Then we come to technological progress. The basic discoveries of science are presumably exogenous; to some extent the findings of technological research depend on them. In economics the content of technological progress must have a wider ambit. We are concerned with what is actually done, with the new methods of production in fact put into operation. The rate at which advantage is taken of availabilities will depend in part on the quality of entrepreneurs; and on Keynes's 'animal spirits', to which we have referred in another connection. How much expenditure on research and development will they judge it worth their while to authorise? There is the possibility of a 'virtuous circle' here. If the government authorities give an undertaking that they will take the measures necessary to raise demand in accordance with the growth potential of the economy, and if there is confidence in this 'undertaking', more will be spent on research and development than otherwise would be, and this in turn will raise the growth potential of the economy. The amount of technological progress, and thereby the rate of increase of the growth potential of the economy, will depend on the intelligence, imagination and competence of the entrepreneurs. It thus depends on whether the institutional structure of industry is such as to enable the right people to be in positions in which they can take the relevant decisions. Zeal and ambition are also needed. It has often been averred that the widespread prevalence of the 'family business' in the U.K. during the nineteenth century was a source of weakness – although that was a period of great economic progress. The family name was a source of zeal and ambition, although there might be the occasional 'ne'er do well'. It is not so clear what the motive force is in the minds of the great impersonal giants who manage our multi-national corporations.

The embodiment of technological progress also requires an increase in skilled workers at all levels. Their shortage may reduce the growth potential of the economy. This brings us back to the educational policy of the country.

I will next set out another variant of the fundamental equation.

$$G_n = \frac{s_o}{C_r} \quad \ldots\ldots\ldots\ldots \quad (3)$$

G_n is the 'natural' rate of growth. One may think of it as growth in accordance with the potential of the economy, or as the maximum possible rate of growth, subject to all that has been said about the balance between work and leisure. The G.D.P. is not a good measure of the rate of growth. It does not have a component showing the increase of welfare due to increased leisure. The goods provided by the government are probably underweighted, since their weights are determined by cost without profit. The gain of welfare due to legal vetoes, e.g. in relation to the preservation of the countryside, is not represented. If this gain is greater than the gain that would have accrued through increased production in the absence of the vetoes, this means that the actual growth rate is greater than that which would have occurred in the absence of the vetoes; but our way of measuring the G.D.P. entails that its increase is less than it would have been without the vetoes.

It is expedient to turn around equation 3 on the principle that the term on the left-hand side is the determinand and those on the right-hand side the determinants:

$$s_o = G_n \cdot C_r \quad \dots\dots\dots\dots \quad (3a)$$

In equation 2 'warranted' growth is, in part, determined by what, amid all the institutional arrangements, which vary so much from country to country and from time to time, people desire to save. It may be regarded as the equation specifying the determinants of growth in a regime of *laissez-faire* capitalism. This is in line with classical economics. What people choose to save, subject to the various institutional arrangements, which differ so much from country to country and from time to time, determines the growth rate of the economy. But in equation 3a the savings ratio is the servant, not the master. It assumes that the 'natural' growth rate is determined by population increase and technological progress, and specifies what saving ratio is required in consequence of that. It is up to the authorities to ensure that this amount of saving is made. I have called equation 2 a specification of what happens under *laissez-faire* capitalism. Does equation 3a imply socialism? I would suggest not. In the spectrum of countries ranging from individualism to socialism, the U.S.A. may be regarded as being at or near the individualist end. But even in that country 'monetary' and 'fiscal' policies are regarded as legitimate weapons of government, including the central bank. These policies serve to doctor the saving ratio and to provide enough, neither more nor less, to maintain reasonably full employment and growth in accordance with the growth potential of the economy. Fiscal policy does this by supplementing (or subtracting from) what people choose to save. Monetary policy, designed to make borrowing from banks or other financial institutions easier (or more difficult), causes more (or less) orders to be placed than otherwise would be, and this by standard (Keynesian) macro-statics causes residual company profit and saving to be higher (or lower) than it would otherwise be. Thus we have, without becoming socialist, weapons for implementing equation 3a and causing saving to be at the level that is required by the growth potential of the economy. In some less developed countries, where private saving is low, and too low in relation to their growth potential, it is very important that fiscal policy should be used to hoist the saving ratio.

There is an implication in equation 3a that there is an optimum rate of saving which the authorities should seek, as a long-term policy, to secure. Reference was made to the U.S. acceptance of the need for monetary and fiscal policies. It is not yet quite clear whether predominant American opinion holds that these weapons should be used to keep the saving ratio at the right level in the long period, or confines the idea of their appropriate use to ironing out the business cycle. That is important; but it implies too narrow a view of the duties of the authorities.

In the normal course of things, we may expect consumption to rise in a progressive economy. There could be phases when inventions were so numerous and capital-intensive that optimal saving rose more in absolute amount than output, thus entailing a decline of consumption; such phases would presumably be extremely rare. But one could get a similar problem owing to a change of government, e.g. if a capitalist country went socialist, or, on a less drastic hypothesis, if a government came into power that was more planning-minded than its predecessor. It might reckon that the capital equipment of the country was below its optimal level. To remedy this situation, the saving ratio would have to be stepped up above its normal level temporarily. For how long? Michal Kalecki discusses this problem in his magis-terial work.[1]

He postulates that one should not let the level of consumption drop while the extra capital is being created; he proposes, humanely, that one should even allow it to continue to rise, but at a sub-normal rate, until the backlog is made good. He had practical experience of such matters in the economic planning of Poland. He holds that the length of time over which a sub-normal increase of consumption should be spread is a matter for arbitrary decision by the government; in this he shows his socialist hand. In fact there is a strictly economic criterion; we have to bring into the calculation the elasticity of the marginal utility of income schedule, and the decline in the marginal utility of income through time, owing to rising income; this will be discussed in a later chapter.

In the equation for warranted growth (G_w), a constant value for G_w is conjugated with constant values for the desired saving ratio (S_d) and the required capital ratio (C_r), or, alternatively, with changing values in those that offset each other. It is often held that, with rising income, the desired saving ratio increases. Historical evidence does not confirm this hypothesis clearly. If the desired saving ratio does indeed rise with rising income, then (assuming constant C_r) the warranted growth rate must be accelerating. It is not likely that the growth in the supply potential of the economy (G_n) can accelerate indefinitely through time. Actual growth (G) cannot, except during phases of recovery from underemployment or from under-use of available technology, exceed G_n; accordingly, if the saving ratio is rising, actual growth must recurrently fall below war-ranted growth. This gives rise to problems, which are discussed in Chapter 7.

A continuing increase in the required capital output ratio (C_r) is conjugated with a deceleration in the warranted growth rate. Rather a paradox! Capital intensity increasing, and, by consequence, growth rate declining. Yet the basic equation shows that.

Some, nurtured in old-fashioned economics, might argue that, if the propensity to save were rising, this, via a fall in the rate of

[1] *Introduction to the Theory of Growth in a Socialist Economy* (Oxford: Basil Blackwell, 1969) [first published in Polish, 1963].

interest, would increase the capital/output ratio in equal proportion, and thus leave the warranted growth rate unchanged, with the economy growing at constant velocity. This is quite unacceptable. We have still to consider the determinants of the interest rate (or rather, of the spectrum of interest rates). It is not denied, and indeed, must be stressed, that the value of C_r depends on the interest rate. It cannot be affirmed that there are 'natural forces' at work, via the interest rate, to keep G_w at a constant value. Whether we regard G_w, or not, as an 'equilibrium' value – that depending on questions relating to the actual 'behavioural parameter' of entrepreneurs – a constant value of G_w has no more claim to be an equilibrium position in a dynamic system than a growing or declining value of it. Accordingly there is no reason why interest rates, supposing them to have some magical property of restoring equilibrium, should cause C_r to rise (or fall) proportionately to any increase (or decrease) in the saving ratio, thereby holding the velocity of the growth rate (G_w) constant.

The tools of static economics, including those of Keynesian macro-statics, are just inadequate to cope with the theory of dynamics.

3 Instability Principle

It is needful to open this chapter by some rather trite remarks. This is because there have been references in the writings of distinguished economists to the 'Harrod knife-edge'. Nothing that I have ever written (or said) justifies this description of my view.

From the first formulation of the growth equation I have argued that the 'warranted' growth rate appearing there, which pertains to *laissez-faire* capitalism, is in 'unstable equilibrium'. This is an expression derived from elementary mechanics. If a marble reposes at the bottom of a bowl, and a force is applied propelling it in a certain direction, it may be made to move up one side of the bowl. Then, if the force ceases to be applied, it will return to its previous position at the bottom of the bowl. It may be said to be in stable equilibrium at the bottom of the bowl. I return unashamedly to school lessons. A billiard ball lying stationary on a billiard table is said to be in neutral equilibrium. If pushed, so that it rolls to a different position, it will have no tendency to return to its old position. But it will not move from its old position further than the force pushes it. It will stay put in the new position. By contrast if a force is applied to a marble resting on top of an inverted bowl, it will depart further from its initial position than the force alone would take it. Its undisturbed repose before the force was applied would be a case of unstable equilibrium. The amount of force needed to shift a body in unstable equilibrium depends on friction, air resistance, etc. The example of the marble on top of the bowl is, perhaps, not happily chosen for my argument; its poise is not altogether unlike being on a knife-edge! A better example would be a ball lying on a grassy slope. It might take quite a hard kick to move it. But, once moved, it might go far further, especially if the hill was steep, than an initial kick of equal force would have moved it if it had been lying in a flat field. It might go the whole way down a mountainside.

Being on a knife-edge is an extreme case of unstable equilibrium. I never suggested that the warranted growth rate had an extreme instability of this sort. On the contrary in my first formulation (*Economic Journal*, March 1939), I suggested, merely by way of example, that the 'reaction time for an accretion or depletion of capital goods to exert its influence upon the flow of orders might be six months. One cannot be said to be on a knife-edge, if it takes six months to move one! (Actually, while perhaps a knife-edge suggests too short a period, my example of a possible reaction time of six months was on the long side in relation to cyclical movements.)

I have to protest against the knife-edge nomenclature, because it sounds utterly unrealistic and even a trifle ridiculous, and might distract the reader's mind from giving serious attention to what I have to say about instability.

We return to the warranted growth equation. Let us suppose that for a period an economy is actually growing at its warranted rate and that then a deviation occurs. Obviously this could happen very easily. The actual rate depends on the aggregate of orders placed at a given time by comparison with the aggregate of orders placed previously. This aggregate is the resultant of decisions by numerous (thousands of) entrepreneurs in consequence of their estimates of the prospects of their own business. The entrepreneurs in question include not only those in charge of manufacturing, but also others all along the line to shopkeepers. All the time they have to make their assessments in the face of great uncertainties, both as regards the likely behaviour, zooming or slumping, of the whole economy and as regards the specific behaviours of the sections in which they are interested.

It would be almost a miracle if the aggregate of decisions resulted in an actual growth rate equal to the 'warranted' growth rate. There are likely to be some deviations all the time. But if they are of moderate dimensions, I would not suppose that they would bring the instability principle into operation. That is why I so much object to the knife-edge idea. It requires a fairly large deviation, such as might be caused by a revision of assessments across the board in some important industry, like the motor car industry, to produce a deviation sufficient to bring the instability principle into play.

Let us suppose there to be a deviation from the warranted growth rate and that $G > G_w$. By the truism it is inevitable that either $s > s_d$ or $C < C_r$ or both. In either case there will be an increase in orders, which will take actual growth still further above the warranted level. Let us take each case in turn.

The increment of savings may occur in the area of persons or companies or both. If, or to the extent that, it occurs in the personal area, persons, finding their savings in excess of what they need, will tend to increase their purchases, which will work back through the chain of intermediaries and cause an increase of orders for the production of goods and services. If it occurs in the area of companies, they will decide either to increase their distribution to shareholders, in which case the effect will be the same as an initial increase in personal savings, or to place extra orders themselves, which they had hitherto been restrained from doing by insufficient profit. Thus, both persons and companies will tend to increase orders, if there is a deviation upwards of actual from warranted growth. The arguments apply in reverse. If there is a chance slip-down of the actual below the warranted growth rate, orders will tend to decline, (or to increase less than they otherwise would have done), and this will reduce the actual still further below the warranted growth rate.

To take the second case: if $C < C_r$, it is obvious that there will be an increase of orders. Fixed capital or stocks in hand being insufficient for needs, the rate of ordering for more will be stepped up. Conversely, if $C > C_r$, there will be redundant equipment or stocks in hand, and this will tend to cause an abatement in the rate of increase of new orders.

I have never been able to satisfy myself in an analysis of how far the ball will roll, of the limits of the region of centrifugal forces surrounding the warranted growth path. In the area above the warranted rate, we come eventually to the ceiling of full employment. This ceiling is a spongy one, since in certain circumstances the 'participation rate' may rise above its normal level. Women, or others not normally employed, may take jobs. It is not likely that *real* wages will be supernormal at ultra-high employment; but there may well be a price inflation that induces those not normally in jobs to seek employment, in order to sustain the family standard of living.

The actual growth rate may be damped before the ceiling of full employment, however defined, is reached, owing to increasing immobility of labour at the margin. In a boom, regional growth rates are likely to be different from each other, and industry growth rates also, so that filling the jobs on offer may entail migration within the country or a change of trade. Although a firm may be able to sell more than it is producing at a point of time, the price elasticity of the demand for its product may not be small enough for it to be able to load the cost of attracting extra labour into its price without knocking off too much of the existing demand. It must be remembered that the marginal cost of attracting labour from other regions or industries is not the higher wage for the extra labour required, but the marginal outlay due to the rise in wages offered, which is much greater. Marginal outlay includes the cost of the higher wages that have to be paid to those already in the employment of the firm.

A classic instance of attracting labour from another region was that of Morris Motors in Oxford in the 1920s, when William Morris (later Lord Nuffield) offered what seemed at the time to be fantastically high wages, in order to attract unemployed Welsh coalminers to his works at Oxford. This was a period of quite heavy unemployment in Britain. There may well have been other firms with jobs going begging, which just could not afford to offer as high wages, in order to attract labour from other regions, as could the ebullient Morris Motors. When the deeper slump came, and some were thrown out of work even by Morris, most of the Welsh coalminers returned to Wales, although unemployment was much heavier there than in Oxford. They preferred Wales to Oxford.

Thus, when there are substantial regional or industrial disparities in growth rates, the feasible overall increase in actual growth may drop and fall below the warranted growth before full employment is reached.

What determines the bottom when the actual rate moves downwards, in accordance with the instability principle? This is a more difficult problem. There were economists around 1931 who thought that there was no 'bottom' and that the capitalist system had gone phut.

This intellectual question has lost practical urgency now,

because, since the war, it has been an established doctrine of political economy that the governmental authorities shall activate monetary and fiscal policies to check a downslide of significant magnitude. This has been done.

However the great slump of 1929–32 did reach its bottom. Both the U.K. and the U.S.A. applied restorative monetary policies in 1932, and it could be argued that it was these measures that actually stopped a further downslide into the pit of hell. President Roosevelt also took steps in 1934, which in retrospect we might regard as measures of 'fiscal' policy, but undesignedly. He authorised very large governmental expenditures and borrowed money to implement them. That is expansionist 'fiscal policy'. It would not have been expansionist, or have been very much less so, if he had financed all his projects out of increased taxation. It is understood that he thought that it would have been very much better if he had financed them out of increased taxation, and did not do so only under the *force majeure* of circumstances. That means that he was not intentionally implementing what we now call an expansionist fiscal policy, which depends essentially on the government financing its extra expenditures on borrowed money.

Nonetheless some, with a feel for economic history, may believe that the great slump would have eventually reached bottom on its own without the application of monetary and fiscal restoratives.

It is needful to advance the postulate that the warranted growth rate itself (G_w) changes under the influence of boom or slump. We will call the initial warranted rate, as pertaining in a steady advance, the 'normal' warranted rate, and the others special warranted growth rates (see also below). As personal incomes go down, people may in due course resist a reduction of consumption below a certain point and decide to scrap savings projects. The saving ratio desired (s_d) would go down and this would have the effect of reducing G_w. With diminished prospects, companies may think it pointless to retain as much undistributed profit as before, and at the same time they will be anxious not to reduce their rates of dividend more than they can help. This will have the effect of reducing the s_d of companies and thereby G_w. These forces could cause the 'special' warranted rate in due course to drop below the actual rate, and the scene would then be set for revival. Furthermore, governmental authorities with fairly rigid expenditure programmes, which would, owing to the reduced yield of taxes, have participated in the *de facto* squeeze on savings due to the fall of G below G_w, might decide to impose extra taxes. This would reinforce the disposition of persons and companies to revise their savings targets (S_d) downwards.

It is needful to say something about the signs of the magnitudes in the fundamental equation. Since the war the actual growth rate of national income as a whole has seldom had a negative value in advanced countries, although 'industrial production' has declined from time to time. In the general approach provided by the fundamental equation, G relates to national income as a whole.

If there is a recession in total national income, so that G (actual) becomes negative, the denominator of C (actual) automatically becomes negative, and thereby also the value of the right-hand term in the truistic equation.

It seldom happens that actual *s* (the saving ratio) becomes negative. This may have happened in the U.S.A. in the worst days of the 1929–33 slump. If it does so, the numerator of C becomes negative simultaneously, on the basis that saving is necessarily equal to investment. Thus a change from a positive to a negative saving ratio leaves the negative sign of the right-hand expression unchanged. In determining whether G is above or below G_w *algebraic* values must be used.

In the fundamental equation C is defined as *net* capital formation. From the value of new fixed capital coming into existence has to be subtracted not only the value of the concurrent reduction of stocks, but also the value of previously existing fixed capital that is not replaced. This value must be reckoned by the cost of replacement of the fixed capital at current prices and not by the 'historic' cost of its production at an earlier date. If the slump is sufficiently severe, net capital formation (and thereby the saving ratio) could become negative.

If the rate of recession (the negative value of G) remains constant, the proportion of existing equipment that is no longer needed each year remains constant also. But if there is an abatement in the *de facto* rate of recession, for example by the increasing resistance of consumers to a decline in their standard of living, as suggested above, the proportion of existing equipment that needs to be replaced goes up. This has the effect of raising the (algebraic) value of C, and thereby lowering that of G_w. That is another factor that could make the decline of the current special G_w overtake that of G.

An arithmetic example may be given on simple lines and with exaggerated values. From what replacements would be with $G = 0$, subtract the value of the capital that can can be stood off and not replaced owing to the negative value of G. We may represent replacements with G continuing to be equal to 0 by the reciprocal of the length of life of the equipment:

TABLE 3.1

Constant linear fall p.a. of national income by 10 per cent of its value at t_0

(a) Replacement required to maintain capital at its level at t_0 as fraction of total capital in each category		(b) Capital outstanding at t_0 that need not be replaced as fraction of total capital in each category	(c) Residual replacement requirement $= ((a) - (b))$
		1st year	
Capital with length of life of 10 years	$\frac{1}{10}$	$\frac{1}{10}$	0
Ditto 9 years	$\frac{1}{9}$	$\frac{1}{10}$	$\frac{1}{90}$
Ditto 8 years	$\frac{1}{8}$	$\frac{1}{10}$	$\frac{1}{40}$
Ditto 1 year	1	$\frac{1}{10}$	$\frac{9}{10}$
		2nd year (assuming action in first year indicated in (c))	
Capital with length of life of 10 years	$\frac{2}{10}$	$\frac{2}{10}$	0
Ditto 9 years	$\frac{1}{9} + \frac{1}{10}$	$\frac{2}{10}$	$\frac{1}{90}$
Ditto 8 years	$\frac{1}{8} + \frac{1}{10}$	$\frac{2}{10}$	$\frac{1}{40}$
Ditto 1 year	$1 + \frac{1}{10}$	$\frac{2}{10}$	$\frac{9}{10}$

The word *minus* appears between columns (a) and (b); the brace structure indicates (a) minus (b).

TABLE 3.2

Fall of national income by 10 per cent in first year and by 5 per cent in second year

	(a)	minus	(b)	=	(c)
			2nd year (assuming action		
Capital with length of life			in first year indicated in Table 3.1)		
of 10 years	$\frac{2}{10}$		$\frac{15}{100}$		$\frac{1}{20}$
Ditto 9 years	$\frac{1}{9} + \frac{1}{10}$		$\frac{15}{100}$		$\frac{11}{180}$
Ditto 8 years	$\frac{1}{8} + \frac{1}{10}$		$\frac{15}{100}$		$\frac{3}{40}$
Ditto 1 year	$1 + \frac{1}{10}$		$\frac{15}{100}$		$\frac{19}{20}$

It is evident, from this illustration in simple arithmetic, that an abatement in the rate of recession gives the need for replacement an absolute upward lift of substantial importance. This raises the concurrent C_r. This is an additional force pulling down the special G_w, since an (algebraic) increase in C_r reduces G_w.

At the bottom of the recession (if it does normally reach a 'bottom') the special warranted growth rate will have the same value as the actual growth rate. It might at first be thought that this is a sort of equilibrium alternative, to that which exists when G_w is 'normal'. But this is not so. This position at the bottom of the slump will not normally be an equilibrium one at all – not even one of 'unstable' equilibrium.

In the basic equation specifying the normal warranted growth rate, it is implied that disturbances will occur only if there are, on the overall average, plus or minus miscalculations of important magnitude about the uncertain future. If there are no such deviations, G_w can be maintained to the satisfaction of all, unless or until changes occur, in the fundamental determinants of G_w, e.g. in the overall average of the capital intensity of technological inventions or of the overall average of the capital intensity of the goods that people want to buy with their successive increments of income in the progress of time.

But at the bottom of a slump there will usually be forces at work tending to continue thereafter to change the value of G_w quite apart from the fundamental determinants just mentioned.

Some of the entirely different forces that tend to reduce the special G_ws during a recession have already been mentioned. If these forces suffice to reduce the gap between the successive special G_ws and the successive actual Gs, this will reduce the rate at which the actual Gs decline through time. The actual Gs will cease to decline when the value of the current actual G is no longer below the value of the current special G_w (bottom of the slump). This point should normally be represented in a time chart by a horizontal curve for G, namely the bottom of a U-shaped curve – this follows from the definition of the bottom of a slump – with the curve showing the successive values through time of the special G_ws intersecting it downwards. The time chart of the special G_w curves will usually continue to fall after the bottom of the slump, until the rise of the G curve, representing actual incomes, begins to reverse the tendencies that had been previously reducing the specific G_ws, e.g. owing to decisions by consumers in impoverished circumstances that they no longer wished to save as high a fraction of their income as they had been saving before.

It has to be admitted, as a theoretical possibility, that it could happen that the temporal chart of the successive special G_ws became horizontal at the precise moment when the gap between it and the G curve was reduced to zero and the G curve consequently became horizontal. That would be a highly unlikely coincidence. If it happened, the economy could continue to bump along the bottom indefinitely. One would have fortuitously got an equilibrium analogous to that defined by the equation for normal warranted growth.

But, happily, like the latter, it would be an unstable equilibrium. It would also be exposed to the centrifugal forces due to an overall average miscalculation as regards the uncertain future of substantial magnitude. If this erred on the side of pessimism, there would be a renewed bout of progressive recession. We should not have reached 'the bottom' after all. This seems to have happened on occasions. 'We thought that we had reached the bottom, but it turned out that we had not!' If the miscalculation was on the side of optimism, then the scene would be set for progressive revival.

It must be repeated that the eventuality of the temporal curve of successive special G_ws becoming flat at the precise moment when it falls to the level of the G curve (when that would be horizontal) would be a highly improbable coincidence, and we do not need to worry much about it.

The phenomenon of the business cycle is one aspect of the growth process. There is something rather peculiar about it, and it had been attracting the attention of economists for more than a century before I wrote anything. One would expect deviations from a steady growth rate; but in the business cycle there does seem to be a cumulative process, continuing by its own momentum, both in the upward and downward phases.

In my studies conducted many years ago I was not, as a theoretical economist, much impressed by the various alleged causes of it, as expounded from Tooke, through Bagehot, to Pigou. Then suddenly I saw light – it was a very vivid experience occurring on a particular day (I so well remember that day, even where I was standing at the moment in my rooms in Christ Church) – and published my theory in a book entitled *The Trade Cycle: an Essay* (1936). That book was written with great speed, and was simply an attempt to put on paper for economists in the shortest possible compass, my central idea – the interaction of J. M. Clark's accelerator with Kahn's 'multiplier'. Keynes to the end refused to be interested in J. M. Clark's accelerator. The Japanese translation of *The Trade Cycle* is still selling merrily in Japan. In that book there are to be found many of the ideas that have been developed in my subsequent writings on dynamic economics. But I did not, when writing it, have the advantage of having in my mind my fundamental growth equation, which also came to me in a flash on a particular day. I recall a kindly Russian enquiring by what process of research and reflection I had evolved my growth equation. Not so. 'Reflection' is, I suppose, relevant. In the course of my 'reflections' I suddenly saw it in a split second. That was not in my Oxford study, but in John Betjeman's cottage in Berkshire, which he lent me in July 1938.

Among the traditional theories of the business cycle, that of alternating psychological business optimism and pessimism alone, in my judgement, has validity. (Harvest cycles – was Jevons right in thinking them moon-induced? – play a diminishing part in the business cycles of advanced countries.) But what causes prevailing phases of optimism and pessimism? One may grant that they are infectious. But, if there is no basic cause for either, why does not one man's optimism cancel the other's pessimism, leaving no net source of infection?

But, if there is in fact an independent basic cause (the instability principle) leading to a cumulative upward or downward process, then the psychological optimism (or pessimism) induced by it may cause the cumulative upward (or downward) movement to be greater than it would otherwise have been.

The 'instability principle', although important in relation to the business cycle, is only a small part of the growth theory that I have endeavoured to expound, and, obviously, only a small part of the growth theory that will eventually be set forth as established doctrine in economic textbooks. And it is only a small part of what can be learned from a study of the fundamental growth equation.

One final point remains to be made in relation to the instability principle. Neo-classical economists have, if I understand aright, sought to show that, if there is a deviation from equilibrium growth, there must be some price mechanism that restores the equilibrium. This is by analogy with the processes in the field of micro-statics, by which, if there is over-production or under-production of a particular commodity, the consequent fall or rise in its price restores its production to its equilibrium level. In fact the processes involved in growth are entirely different from those of micro-statics.

The price relied on by some to restore the warranted growth rate is the rate (constellation of rates) of interest. It is a fact that the rate of interest tends to rise in booms and to fall in slumps.

In a boom (upward departure from the warranted growth rate), either savings will be redundant to what persons and companies feel they want to make, or real capital in hand will be less than producers (and merchants) feel that they currently require, or (more probably) both. Excess saving will tend to cause savers to offer more capital disposal in the market than usual; deficient real capital in hand will tend to cause those who use real capital to bid for more capital disposal than usual. A rise in the market rate of interest implies that the excess saving is less than the deficiency of real capital.

We are discussing the matter in neo-classical terms. According to Keynesian theory the rise of interest that occurs in a boom is due to something quite different, namely the failure of the authorities to raise the rate of the increase of the money supply by as much as the rise in the rate of increase of the put-through of goods in the boom multiplied by the rate of inflation that may be occurring.

To return to the classical concept, it is held that the rise in the rate of interest will stimulate the offer of capital disposal and depress the demand for it, thereby bringing the two into equality. But this does not imply that the growth rate returns to its warranted level. On the contrary, it will stay above it. There is no return to the previous equilibrium. Savings will be more than they were before and so will orders for real capital. Thus we have something entirely different from the tendency to return to an equilibrium position as demonstrated in micro-statics.

At this point a word may be said about the influence of the rate of interest. It appears to me to be very doubtful whether a rise in it has any appreciable tendency to increase the savings of persons or companies in a relatively short period. In the cumulative process of an upward departure of actual growth from warranted growth we are dealing with a comparatively short period. Persons have their well thought-out saving plans – their insurance premiums, etc. They do not modify them every few months in response to interest rate changes. Furthermore, it is by no means certain in what direction the modification would be, if there were one. As is well known, a rise in the rate of interest may cause them to save less than they otherwise would. Their demand for retirement pensions or money to leave to their children may be inelastic. If a person's income goes up in a boom, he may think that he would like to add k pounds to his retirement pension. The higher the rate of interest the less money this will cost, so that the rise in the rate of interest, if it occurs, causes him to save less than he otherwise would.

Companies are on both sides of the market as regards capital disposal. If the boom makes them short of real capital, they may well distribute less (save more) than they otherwise would. It does not seem likely that many companies would actually reduce dividends during a boom in profit. But, while their own requirements may make them conservative in their distribution, it does not seem likely that a rise in the market rate of interest would by itself cause them to distribute less than they would otherwise have done.

Finally we come to the effect of a high rate of interest on their plans for adding to their real capital. It is to be remembered that for most (almost all) firms the capital market is an imperfect one. If the higher interest is associated with increased difficulty of borrowing from normal sources of supply of capital disposal to them, this may indeed limit their plans for real capital formation. Whether or not there is in these conditions an increased difficulty of borrowing from usual sources will depend largely on what the monetary authorities do about the money supply. Discussion of this would take us into Keynesian territory, which is *verboten* in a discussion of the neo-classical theory.

Those who argue that the equilibrium of the warranted growth path is not unstable appear to rely on the idea that high interest will cause a change in the mix in which capital and labour are employed in the processes of production (and distribution) in favour of the use of labour. This idea is unplausible in the highest degree. It is to be remembered that the rise of interest due to an upward deviation of the actual from the warranted rate of growth is a fairly short-period phenomenon; when the actual rate returns to the warranted rate, the rate of interest will presumably return to where it was before. In assessing the costs of alternative methods of production, firms often have some standard rate of profit, which includes interest, that they add to the input costs. It is most unlikely that they will modify this standard rate in accordance with short term variations in the market rate of interest. Of course if the market rate of interest rises considerably and stays up for a substantial period, as it has done recently (1971), that may cause firms to increase the mark-up. But even when they do this, it is seldom likely to have any appreciable effect on their decision about which method of production among alternative methods with different capital-labour mixes is the most efficient. Interest is not a sufficiently important element in cost.

It is true that there may be very large differences in the labour-capital mix as between small firms and large and as between different countries and different periods of time. These are due to differences of technological availabilities or to market sizes, and not in most cases to differences in the rate of interest. In the late nineteenth century the U.S.A. developed progressively more capital-intensive methods of production than the U.K. although the rate of interest was consistently higher there than in the U.K.

I am confident that the theory that the 'warranted' equilibrium growth rate of *laissez-faire* capitalism, without management or interference, is unstable, stands firm; and that it is the fundamental explanation of the business cycle.

There is the further question of whether *laissez-faire* capitalism tends to bring the economy to a full employment position. It was the central doctrine of Keynes, with which I agree, that this was not so. The actual facts of experience, showing rather lengthy spells of unemployment, also suggest that this is not so. But, even if it were so, that would not guarantee growth in accordance with potential. Producers will not scrap existing methods of production, in favour of methods yielding greater output per person, if they do not expect the lower price to stimulate demand sufficiently to absorb the extra output. So, even with full employment, the growth potential may not be achieved.

4 Capital Output Ratio

The capital-output ratio is an expression increasingly used in economic literature, but not always unambiguously. The provision of a precise definition is not an altogether easy task. One may approach it by first considering the kindred concept of the capital-labour ratio.

In this expression labour is taken to cover, not only the wage-earning factor, but current inputs into the productive process of all kinds. We may approach this by considering the more general concept of the capital intensity of productive processes.

There are two principal methods for measuring capital intensity, which we may call the Austrian and the Marxist respectively. The two methods should give the same ordering for the degrees of capital intensity, whether in the comparison of various products at a given point of time, of the methods of production of a given commodity at different points of time, or of alternative available methods of producing a given commodity at a given time.

By the Austrian method there is no 'ratio'. One measures capital intensity by taking the average interval of time between all the various inputs of productive resources and the outputs which they are designed to produce. The greater the time interval, the more capital intensive is the method of production said to be.

If fixed capital is used, the inputs required to produce that capital must be included in the calculation of the average time interval; that indeed is of the essence of this method. The time interval between the application of resources to the production of fixed capital and the eventuation of the product that it is designed to make will presumably normally be larger than the interval between the labour that uses the fixed capital and the output. Thus if the amount of fixed capital used in method A for producing a given object is greater than that in method B, the time interval is likely to be longer.

There is the traditional distinction in political economy between the kind of input that produces one single particular object only and that which yields a flow of objects. Accordingly, to get an accurate assessment of the average time interval in the latter case, it is needful to be able to project correctly for how long the flow of outputs due to a given input will continue to come in. That difficulty arises with other methods of measurement also.

Some have objected in principle to the time-interval concept on the ground that it involves an infinite regress. The machinery that extracts coal has had to be produced with steel and that steel had to be produced with the aid of coal, which in its turn required machinery – or, perhaps, a primitive axe! – to produce it, and so on *ad infinitum*. This objection is not really valid. The proportion of current output attributable to inputs in the backward stretch of time is smaller the further one goes back. An infinite diminishing series can be summed.

It must be admitted, however, that the time-interval concept is not very handy for application. Its value is rather that it provides an intellectual clarification. Interest is the reward for waiting. The longer the average waiting between inputs and the output of a given object, the greater will the interest element be in the value of that object.

In what I have called the Marxist approach, we measure capital intensity by a ratio, namely the ratio of embodied labour to living labour. We must, of course, use 'labour' in its broadest sense, namely to include inputs of all kinds. Any useful object, which has been rendered into the shape that it now has by previous inputs, 'embodies' labour. These objects include not only fixed capital, houses, etc., but also goods in process, in transit, and in retail shops, until they are finally destroyed by 'use'. It has been customary to exclude movable objects that have reached the hands of their final buyers – household furniture, trousers in the cupboard, etc. – even although they still have a useful length of life before them. This exclusion may become a little precarious, now that the practice of buying *objets d'art*, not for their enjoyment, but as a hedge against inflation, has become so widespread.

In all cases capital must be given its written-down value during the production process. Thus, if an object has already done half the useful work that it is expected to do, then it must be reckoned as embodying half the labour that was used to create it. Accordingly this method of measuring capital intensity also requires insight into the future. Doubtless in accountancy practice arbitrary, and, usually, conservative, rates of depreciation are used. But this has no bearing on our present analysis.

In order to give a figure for the amount of 'living' labour, we have to select some arbitrary time period. A year is generally used. Thus the amount of living labour is said to be all the inputs during the course of the year. These include those devoted to creating new capital or replacing worn out capital.

As the inputs are of different kinds, their relative values have to be established, in order to get the amount of living input required for a particular product or for the national income. As regards labour embodied before the period under consideration, the various kinds of inputs may have had relative values at the time when they were embodied different from their present ones. Strictly speaking, in assessing the total value of embodied labour, the old inputs should be revalued in accordance with their present values. A formidable task! Happily in C, to which I shall in due course return, we are concerned only with the increment of embodied labour during the period, so that no problem of revaluation arises. The concept of the total value of the capital in the country, often designated by K, is statistically unmanageable, and I have not used it in my fundamental growth theory. But in the work of some writers it occupies a prominent place.

It is to be stressed that the capital-labour ratio is a useful weapon for comparing alternative methods of producing a given object, for comparing methods of producing different objects or for comparing the changes through time of methods of producing a given object. It is on the whole an unserviceable tool in relation to national income as a whole, but it can be employed in a very rough sort of way for comparing different countries.

A word must be said here about land and mineral deposits. In traditional economics these were kept separate from 'capital', advisedly in my opinion. There was also the classic distinction between the value of land as determined by the 'natural and indestructible powers of the soil' and that due to past improvements. The distinction is absolutely unmanageable. And that gives a further reason for keeping K right out of the fundamental growth equations. But there is no insuperable difficulty in assessing the amount of labour that has been embodied in land improvement in the current period, as required for the assessment of C.

On the other hand, it is proper to include the current contribution of land towards current output among living inputs. This may be paradoxical. But, as already explained, inputs of all kinds in the current periods should be counted as 'living' inputs. The different kinds of living input, from unskilled to managerial labour, etc., have to be valued relatively to each other. The value of the current input that is contributed by rented land may be gauged by the rent. If the land is cultivator-owned, its rentable value may be assessed by analogy. There should be a similar assessment when rents are running below the true economic values owing to long leases.

Thus we may define the capital/labour ratio as

$$\frac{\text{Value of embodied inputs, written down}}{\text{Value of living inputs (including use of land) p.a.}}$$

We may go over to the capital-output ratio. In the case of the capital-labour ratio we saw that it was needful to establish the relative values of the various kinds of input, both living and embodied, and in the case of embodied inputs to revalue them if the relative values of these kinds of inputs had changed since they were embodied. With the capital output ratio we come to a fresh set of problems. The numerator and denominator of the capital labour ratio are aggregates of the same kinds of things – inputs. But the denominator of the capital-output ratio consists of things of an altogether different kind from the inputs, viz. goods and services. We have accordingly to find a common yardstick for measuring the relative values of inputs and outputs.

This brings us to the age-old problem of the best measure of value – a labour measure or a goods measure. The austere school of David Ricardo, and, in our times, Sir Ralph Hawtrey, have desiderated a labour measure. This means that the prices of goods (and services) fall in the economy as a whole in precise proportion to the average increase in the quantity of output per unit of input, i.e. to the average increase in productivity. This implies that the average of the rates of rewards to the various kinds of inputs would remain constant through time. We need not dwell on the still more austere desideratum of Professor F. A. von Hayek, that prices should move down in proportion, not to the increase of output per head, but to the increase of total output in a given economy, so that with increasing population the fall of prices would be proportionately greater than it would otherwise have been. This would mean a continuing fall through time of the money rewards to factors of production.

On the more moderate Ricardo–Hawtrey plan, factors with stable money rewards would experience a rising level of real rewards through falling prices.

In these days of endemic inflation, we shall feel happy if we can achieve the target of stable prices, viz. a goods measure of value. Money rewards to factors then rise in proportion to the average overall increase of productivity. Let us proceed in terms of a regime of stable prices.

It is to be noted that the real value of all rewards, including profit, rises in the same proportion as the output of goods and services. In a regime of stable prices the money value of rewards rises in this proportion.

Profit has not so far been discussed. It presents difficulties. It clearly enters into the value of output. Is there an input corresponding to it? Profit clearly does not accrue in return for no service. On the other hand it, or at least part of it, is a residue. This makes it difficult to value the service, for which an unknown reward will ultimately be paid, as and when it is rendered.

One way of dealing with the matter might be to regard the service for which profit is paid – dare we call it enterprise? – as a living input rendered simultaneously with the accrual of the output. Much depends on the area for which we are seeking to establish the capital-output ratio. We have already seen that the concept of the capital labour ratio is not very helpful, if applied to the economy as a whole, owing to the difficulty of assessing the value of K, namely capital as a whole.

But if we are considering a particular firm or industry, which purchases embodied labour from another firm or industry, the value of what is purchased will include profit. Thus some part of all profit will figure in the value of embodied inputs and living inputs of the service for which profit is paid may be reckoned as occurring simultaneously with these purchases. There may be some portion of aggregate profit that cannot be handled in this way or sensibly be included in the capital/labour ratio. But all profit goes into the value of output. Let us call this portion 'residual profit'.

We may define the capital-output ratio as

$$\frac{\text{Value of embodied inputs, written down}}{\text{Value of living inputs} + \text{'residual' profit} - \text{value of replacements}}$$

Replacements have to be subtracted in the denominator, since living inputs devoted to them merely serve to keep the value of embodied inputs, written down, intact. They offset the inputs currently being sweated out of embodied inputs through wear and tear and old age. They do not contribute to an increase of current output. The two ratios may be expected to move together, unless residual profit is advancing at a rate different from that of the other terms.

It is to be noted that the capital-labour ratio is entirely different from the much used concept of value of capital per head, a hybrid notion. In an economy in which output per head was rising one would expect the capital per head ratio to rise also. Professor Sidney Weintraub, however, has presented a surprising statistical computation that seems to show that in the U.S.A., a highly capitalised country, capital per head had a downward trend for more than a decade in the thirties and forties.[1] This means that technical progress in the U.S.A. in this period must have been highly capital-saving. Since, with progress, the value per unit of embodied inputs rises, inventions would have to be substantially capital-saving merely to prevent the value of capital per head from rising.

In fact a reasonable explanation can be given, which is probably correct. It may be that technical progress in the methods of producing fixed capital was in this period more rapid than that in the methods of using it or of providing services. This

[1] S. Weintraub, *Some Aspects of Wage Theory and Policy* (Chilton Co., 1963) p. 106.

would reduce the amount of embodied labour relatively to that of living labour, and, if it reduced it enough, it could reduce the value per head of the working population of all embodied labour despite the continuing rise in value of each unit of embodied labour. Questions of age distribution also come in.

Technical progress may be labour-saving, neutral or capital saving. There is a problem about the best definition of netrality. In my *Towards a Dynamic Economics* (1948) I supplied one. I defined it as one which does not disturb what I have called in these pages the capital–labour ratio and leaves the length of the production process unchanged. I wrote

> ... clearly in a case of this sort there is no question of a correct definition. One's definition should involve a reasonable use of language. As well as being almost essential as a tool for the kind of approach to the dynamic problem which I am attempting, there is much to be said for my definition both on logical and econometrical grounds ... A stream of inventions, which are neutral as defined, will, provided that the rate of interest is unchanged, leave the distribution of the total national product as between labour (in the broadest sense) and capital unchanged. The prevailing character of inventions through a period in which there is no cumulative change in the rate of interest, can be measured by comparing the growth in the value of capital with the growth of income. This can also be done in each industry separately and in each firm.

Then follows a passage about amortisation which is dealt with elsewhere in these pages. I will continue quoting from my earlier work.

In his *Theory of Wages* Mr Hicks supplied a somewhat different definition of a neutral invention (pp. 121–127). He defined it as one which raises the marginal productivity of labour and capital in equal proportions. This commends itself to reason, but there are a number of causes which make it unsuitable for my purpose. The special characters of my definition may be brought out by a comparison with his.

1. The Hicks definition make the neutrality of an invention depend on various elasticities, namely elasticities of

substitution as between capital and labour in other industries and of the demand for other products using them in various proportions, throughout the whole economy. Thus the neutrality of the invention depends on circumstances quite unrelated to the intrinsic character of the invention itself. My definition determines the matter solely by reference to the invention itself, and is, on this account, a handier tool in a first approach to a great field of study, in which the utmost simplicity is desirable.

2. Mr Hicks compares his definition with an earlier one given by Professor Pigou.[1] Pigou's definition makes neutrality depend on what happens on the assumption that the quantities of capital and labour available to the economy are unaffected by the invention. Professor Pigou proceeds to consider, from the point of view of the wider question of the harmony between the interests of 'labour' and society as a whole, what will result if the supply of the factors is altered in consequence; but this analysis is not taken to modify the definition. Mr Hicks seems to leave the question what is to be assumed about the supply of the factors open. But whether he is taken to follow Professor Pigou in assuming absolutely inelastic supply or not, the position is equally unsatisfactory.

To assume an absolutely inelastic supply in every case is somewhat unrealistic. To allow, on the other hand, that the actual elasticities of supply, whatever they may be from time to time, must be taken into account in determining whether an invention is neutral or not, again makes the definition of neutrality depend, not on the intrinsic nature of the invention, but on quite outside factors.

Furthermore either assumption, and indeed this whole method of approach, is quite appropriate in relation to a once-over invention (static analysis), but not to a stream of successive new inventions continuing through time.

In the static scheme of thought it is proper to assume determinate supply schedules of the factors and to conceive of marginal productivities as governed by the intersection of supply and demand curves. A once-over invention leads to a once-over change of prices which determines and is determined by a once-over change in the supply of factors in the

[1] *Economics of Welfare* (2nd ed.) pp. 632–8.

ordinary way, the supply schedules being conceived to remain unchanged.

When we have to consider a stream of new inventions confronting a growth of capital (viz. positive saving continuing to accrue) a different technique is required. We must remember that the equilibrating force may not be, as in the static analysis, a price (or set of prices), but a certain rate of change of price.

3. In selecting an assumption for the purpose of defining neutrality one has to choose between the assumption of a fixed supply of factors or that of an increasing one. The assumption of a constant supply schedule of the old fashioned kind is inappropriate, since that is related to a once-over price change, which has no significance in dynamics; to put it differently, one co-ordinate of the schedule is a price, and not, as is required in dynamics, a rate of change of price.

To assume a constant supply of the factors through time is highly unrealistic in relation to any of the economies in which we are interested, and at the same time sets a much more complicated problem for the definition of neutrality. Thus it may be rejected on two excellent grounds.

As I have chosen to approach the dynamic problem by asking what rate of increase of capital would be consistent with certain rates of increase in other parts of the system, it has seemed simplest to define a neutral stream of inventions as one which shall require a rate of increase of capital equal to the rate of increase of income engendered by it. If the stream of inventions requires capital to increase at a greater rate, then it is labour-saving or capital-requiring; and conversely. The rate of interest is assumed to be constant, since that is a simpler assumption than that of a changing rate of interest.

4. The neutrality of an invention would be determined on my definition by reference to what happens to the capital coefficient, if the rate of interest is constant. In the language of statics this implies an infinitely elastic supply of capital at the existing rate of interest. My definition does not, of course, assume that the supply is infinitely elastic; but if it is, then it will be possible to use it to classify all and sundry inventions as they occur. Those who follow Keynes in holding that,

save in conditions of Full Employment, the supply of capital is in fact infinitely elastic at a given rate of interest, should give my definition a particularly good mark for its econometric soundness.

5. It does not appear possible to say whether Mr Hicks's definition or mine would put more actual inventions into the labour-saving box. His depends partly on the outside circumstances, mine on the intrinsic character of the invention only. I cannot find any consideration making it probable that either his or mine would put more in.

I hope, I may say in digression, already to be giving a dim conception – and I only conceive dimly myself – of the kind of revolution that is required in economics. I want to see those keen tools of thought of Pigou and Hicks, which have been so finely used to perfect static theory, applied to the rough dynamics of Ricardo, changing it indeed out of recognition in the process, as modern marginal analysis has already long since changed the theories of price and cost of Adam Smith and Ricardo. This should involve a considerable re-writing of economics.

It must not be taken to be implied that a neutral invention as defined is the most likely kind of invention. Nothing of this sort is presupposed in my definition, or for that matter in the definitions advanced by others. I might be permitted to observe in passing, however, that it is not my impression that in recent years inventions have been predominantly of a character tending to raise the capital coefficient as calculated at and determined by a constant rate of interest; it is not my impression that inventions have been predominantly labour-saving in the sense defined.

With a stationary population, then, and a steady and neutral technological advance, the new capital required would be a constant fraction of income equal to the increase of income (or output) in any period, considered as a fraction of total income multiplied by the capital coefficient. The same period must be used in calculating the increase of output and in computing the capital coefficient.

If a is the fraction of income required to be saved when population is increasing at a given rate X and technology is stationary and b the fraction of income required to be saved when population is stationary and technological advance makes possible an increase of output at rate Y, then, when there is both a population increase of X and an increase of output per head of Y, the fraction of income required to be saved will be $a + b + ab$. ab is likely to be a very small quantity and may be safely neglected.

If the stream of new inventions and improvements are capital intensive on overall average, this will be conjugated with a lower warranted growth than would obtain if they were neutral. If part of available savings are needed to finance more capital-intensive methods of production, there will not be so much left over to finance sheer expansion as such.

May a given warranted growth rate be associated with unemployment, and even with rising unemployment? It seems so. This question will have to be explored thoroughly, when we examine the interactions, in different circumstances, between the warranted and natural growth rates (Chapter 7). Of the latter the rate of increase in the population of working age is a leading determinant. The instability principle, as explained in the last chapter, relates only to the interactions between the warranted and actual growth rates.

The idea of substantial positive unemployment, in addition to mere frictional unemployment, being present in a condition of equilibrium is, of course, consistent with Keynesian macro-statics. But according to dynamic theory the pool of unemployment is not likely to remain stagnant for long. Something is likely to happen to cause an upward departure of the actual from the warranted growth rate. The economy will move towards the ceiling of full employment; it may not get the whole way there for reasons set out in the last chapter. In many cases – depending on the relation between the warranted and actual rates – the condition of full employment, if achieved, may be highly unstable. This is not only required by dynamic theory, but also seems conformable with much experience in capitalist econo-mies. This has nothing whatever to do with wages being in-flexible downwards, a doctrine of old-fashioned micro-statics. Keynes was right in holding, in his macro-static theory, that a downward revision of wages would not, to any important degree, tend to reduce unemployment.

There remains the question of what determines the relative values of the various living inputs. Here traditional micro-statics stands in good stead. There are the market-place forces of supply and demand, which, if unimpeded, secure a Pareto optimum. The result of their interplay may be modified by monopolistic conditions. In dynamics we have to consider whether the degree of monopoly is growing or stationary. There is a third force, in my opinion important, namely historic tradition, which may reflect onto the present, caused by events occurring more than a century ago. There have in the long past been established certain rules, by which, if craftsman A was then deemed to deserve a 10 per cent higher wage than crafts-man B, that differential has been maintained until the present. When the rate of pay of craftsman A goes up, that of craftsman B goes up in the same ratio, whatever the market forces are, or whatever is the monopolistic power of the unions looking after the craft A type of employee, compared with that of those looking after craft B. To the latter will accrue automatic increases of wages, as related to increases in craft A, whatever the market forces or monopoly positions favouring (or dis-favouring) workers in craft B.

C_r relates to the incremental capital output ratio in the equilibrium of warranted growth. It is measured in terms of current values; accordingly it is not affected by post-mortem revaluations of capital assets. If there have been deviations from the equilibrium of warranted growth during the relevant past, this will affect the value of C_r in the manner described in the last chapter.

5 Interest

The classical theory of interest is that it is the price that equates the supply of capital to the demand for it. For greater precision one should substitute for 'capital' above the term 'capital disposal', retaining the word 'capital' to describe physical objects in which inputs have been embodied with a view to future outputs, as already explained.

Some writers have liked to refer also to 'human capital', regarding the work of teachers and trainers as inputs into those taught that will enable them over future time to produce more than they would have been able to do without the education and training in question. We have a regress here too. There is the labour of those who educated the educators, and so on backwards. This is a nice analogy, but of limited serviceableness. It has one important application. It is needful that governments with limited amounts of capital disposal available should ensure that a proper proportion is devoted to education and technological training. But there is this difference, which makes the idea of interest inapplicable in this field: those responsible for inputs of this kind do not themselves usually receive back the values represented by the higher outputs of those educated. This may also apply in certain categories of physical objects, like public parks, etc. Not all education should be regarded as an input of capital disposal. There are those parts of education that teach the recipients to be better and wiser people, to have greater appreciation of the beauties of nature and of art, and to comport themselves in their social relations in ways conducive to peace and harmony; here we are drifting away from the realm of economics proper into that of a wider sociology.

On the demand side those who enter the market want capital disposal in order to be able to finance the embodiment of living inputs into productive capital, the outputs from which will accrue only at later dates. It is easy to see why they are prepared to pay a price for this. There is also a demand for capital disposal for investment in consumer capital. It takes various forms that may be given the generic name of consumer credit (see also below). In this very general discussion of the nature of interest I shall leave aside for the time being the distinctions between the different kinds of borrowing – short-term, medium-term, long-term, etc., and acquiring capital disposal in exchange for equities.

Why is the supplier not content to receive his capital disposal back at a later date, being content with no more than a modest service charge for the transaction? The supplier has a time preference. He is being asked to swap value in hand for value at some future date. He prefers to have value in hand now, and, if asked to sacrifice this in exchange for value in the future, he needs a substantial premium to be induced to do so. Interest is, as already stated, the reward for present abstinence.

There are two aspects of this time preference, which ought to be, but are not always, distinguished sharply. One aspect is what Pigou called 'lack of telescopic faculty'. Persons often cannot envisage the pleasure of having a certain amount of value in hand at some future date as clearly as they envisage the pleasure that they can get for an equal amount of value now. Allied to this is brute appetite. It is a question of the emotions. David Hume said that 'reason is, and ought to be, the servant of the passions'. Whether the 'and ought to be' is appropriate in this context we shall presently discuss.

The other aspect, admirably set forth by Irving Fisher, is the diminishing utility of income. If output per caput in the economy is growing year by year, then persons, on the overall average, will expect to have higher incomes in future years. Swapping a given amount of value now for an equal amount at future dates is not a good bargain for those who expect to have a higher income at those future dates, since at those dates the marginal utility of a pound of income will be lower. An excess of value returned, or returnable, to the supplier of capital disposal over the value that he supplies now is required in order to induce him, if he is rational, to make the swap. That excess is 'interest'. Of course, there are some, like almost all university undergraduates, whom no rate of interest of any amount feasible in more or less developed countries could induce to save part of their incomes for a future accrual. The average student, apart from the minority that inherit large money, assume that in, say, twenty years after graduation they will be getting a much larger income than they now have; it would make no sense for them to cut down on their modest student expenditure in order to add something that will come to them in future years. Apart from business cycles of optimism and pessimism, most human beings are fairly optimistic about their own prospects. There is of course the exceptional type. I have known very distinguished and intellectually significant students who have confided in me that they would never possibly be able to earn money and would very much dislike doing so, if they could. I should suppose this refined type to be a little less rare in the old world than in America; but I am not sure about that – it would be difficult to make a statistical investigation since they are so many more with substantial independent means in the latter country.

There are those in the opposite position, to whom the prospect of a decline of income after earning capacity drops becomes significant. These would save something, even if there were no rate of interest on capital disposal. If this class of persons could alone satisfy all demands for capital disposal then there would be no need for a positive rate of interest. But one has to take the pattern of the whole population. If the weight in the population of those who are still able to foresee a growth of income on balance during their remaining years is greater than that of those who foresee a decline on balance during what remains of their life, a positive rate of interest for capital suppliers will be required by the diminishing utility of income principle.

We must return to the question of consumer credit, now so widely prevalent. It is a question of spreading forward from the present the cost of more or less durable consumer goods that yield enjoyment over a period of time. Many consumers might not be able to afford the whole cost of such goods out of their current income, without digging too deeply into their consumption of perishable goods. It is natural that they should be willing to pay interest for the advantage of not having to pay a down sum for the durable consumer goods. This is independent of whether they expect their incomes to rise, remain stationary or fall during the period in question. Actually, rates of interest in the market for this particular use of capital disposal have often been exorbitant. This is probably because this market is much less ancient than the markets for the capital disposal required for production and trade. In due course, rates charged for consumer credit will doubtless fall under the influence of competition; but these things take time.

Capital disposal is generated by the savings of persons, companies and governmental agencies. It may also come from depreciation funds not used for replacement, as when some particular line of production is terminated. Aggregate investment in an economy is equal to aggregate saving. Banks, as companies, can contribute to saving by not distributing to their shareholders the whole of their realised profit. But they do not add to aggregate saving by increasing their holdings of securities of various kinds or by their loans to clients. There has sometimes been confused thinking on this point.

Banks may encourage investment by becoming more willing to lend to clients, who have been held back from making investments that they had been wanting to make by lack of available finance. It must always be remembered that the capital market is an imperfect one. The central bank normally governs changes towards greater ease or toughness in the willingness of the banks to lend by its own operations, and by the observance by the banks of legal or conventional cash ratios.

To repeat, the banks do not directly generate additional saving by lending more. Their easier attitude to lending, however, may cause some investments to be made that would not otherwise have taken place. But saving must always be equal to investment. A paradox here.

In a steady advance, the increase of total investment, including that financed by bank loans, will proceed concurrently with an equal increase in savings; there is no problem. But suppose an upward inflection in bank lending. Instanter the extra investment financed by the banks will be fully offset by a depletion of stocks, so that there will be no net extra investment in the economy as a whole; those newly employed on the extra investment will spend part of their incomes and this will deplete stocks. But in due course steps will be taken to increase the flow of consumer goods, to match, not only the requirements of those at work on the additional investment, but also the requirements of those producing the extra consumer goods. This is Kahn's

famous 'Multiplier'. The virtuous circle of increased spending
proceeds, until the savings of those newly employed, or working
longer hours, and indeed the extra savings of their employers
also, add up to the value of the extra investment, as encouraged
by the banks, plus that of the extra stocks that may be needed
in relation to the higher level of consumption.

When the banks make money easier, they may not only lend
more to clients, but also purchase bills and bonds. Both processes
necessarily increase the money supply. Both processes involve a
swap of assets between the banks and the non-bank public.
The swap raises the ratio of money to non-money assets held by
the non-bank public.

This brings us straight onto Keynes's theory of interest, a
central feature of his whole system. The increase in the money
supply held by the public will normally be greater than they
require for circulating goods, given a constant velocity of cir-
culation, while their stock of non-money assets will be reduced
below its previous level. They did not ask for this to happen; it
just happened overnight, so to speak, through the action of the
banks. The non-bank public will seek to restore the ratio
between money and non-monetary assets to, or towards, its old
level by bidding for bonds, etc. While some individuals may
achieve what they desire, the non-bank public as a whole
cannot do so, unless or until the banks start moving in the
opposite direction and reduce the money supply. The quantity
of money in the hands of the public has been increased and that
of non-monetary assets has been reduced, and that is that.
Meanwhile the attempts by the non-bank public to restore
their non-bank assets to the desired level will send up the prices
of these assets and thus bring down interest rates. That is the
Keynesian theory of what determines the rate of interest. His
'liquidity preference' concerns the proportion of their total
assets that people want to hold in the form of cash and the
proportion that they want to hold in the form of securities of
different kinds. The banking system determines the proportions
available for holding by the non-bank public. The word 'want'
in 'want to hold' is relative. How strong is their 'want'? They
will want to hold more in the form of securities if their interest
yield is high and less if their interest yield is low. The market
rate of interest moves to the level that makes people want to

hold cash and other assets in proportions equal to those that actually exist.

What then is the relation between the classical theory of interest and the Keynesian theory? At the stage that the theory had reached in Keynes's *Treatise on Money*, the relation is really quite simple. Classical theory specifies the determinants of the rate that is consistent with equilibrium, while his own theory specifies the determinants of the actual market rate from time to time. It is needful to recall that in the *Treatise* saving is not necessarily equal to investment. Keynes was well aware, as he himself stated, of the book-keeping identity of total saving to total investment, as needed, for instance, for national income accounts. He was able to postulate an inequality, as needed for his own equilibrium theory, by excluding from what is saved 'windfall' profit; if a company makes a windfall loss (or subnormal profit) the shortfall in its saving below what it would otherwise have been is subtracted from total national saving in assessing the amount of what we may call Keynesian saving. If in the economy as a whole there are net windfall profits or windfall losses (subnormal profits), that is a symptom of disequilibrium. I quote Keynes.

> Following Wicksell, it will be convenient to call the rate of interest which would cause the second term of our second Fundamental Equation [viz. Investment minus Saving divided by the output of consumer goods] to be zero the *natural-rate* of interest, and the rate which actually prevails the *market-rate* of interest. Thus the natural rate of interest is the rate at which saving and the value of investment are exactly balanced, so that the price-level of output as a whole exactly corresponds to the money-rate of the efficiency earnings of the Factors of Production. Every departure of the market rate from the natural rate tends, on the other hand, to set up a disturbance of the price-level by causing the second term of the second Fundamental Equation to depart from zero.[1]

In the *General Theory* Keynes departs further from the classical position, and also indulges in some unnecessary tilting at classical economics. This may have done some harm to the

[1] *Treatise on Money*, vol. I, pp. 154–5.

progress of economic theory, which should consist of a system of harmonious concepts.

In the *Treatise* there is only one equilibrium position, namely when investment is equal to saving (*Treatise* definition of these concepts). In the *General Theory* Keynes insists that there are many possible positions of equilibrium, with corresponding levels of unemployment. What the actual position of equilibrium at any time is depends on the determinants of aggregate effective demand. But the economy may also be, doubtless usually is, in disequilibrium. The 'natural' rate of interest remains that consistent with equilibrium. But since there are as many possible equilibrium positions as there are levels of unemployment, there are equally many so called 'natural' rates of interest. He writes:

> In my *Treatise on Money* I defined what purported to be a unique rate of interest, which I called the *natural rate* of interest – namely, the rate of interest which, in the terminology of my *Treatise*, preserved equality between the rate of saving (as there defined) and the rate of investment. I believed this to be a development and clarification of Wicksell's 'natural rate of interest', which was, according to him, the rate which would preserve the stability of some, not quite clearly specified, price-level.
>
> I had, however, overlooked the fact that in any given society there is, on this definition, a *different* natural rate of interest for each hypothetical level of employment. And, similarly, for every rate of interest there is a level of employment for which that rate is the 'natural' rate, in the sense that the system will be in equilibrium with that rate of interest and that level of employment. Thus it was a mistake to speak of *the* natural rate of interest or to suggest that the above definition would yield a unique value for the rate of interest irrespective of the level of employment. I had not then understood that, in certain conditions, the system could be in equilibrium with less than full employment.
>
> I am now no longer of the opinion that the concept of a 'natural' rate of interest, which previously seemed to me a most promising idea, has anything very useful or significant to contribute to our analysis. It is merely the rate of interest

which will preserve the *status quo*; and, in general, we have no predominant interest in the *status quo* as such.

If there is any such rate of interest, which is unique and significant, it must be the rate which we might term the *neutral* rate of interest, namely the natural rate in the above sense which is consistent with *full* employment, given the other parameters of the system.[1]

Why all this fuss? And why the wording that tends to pooh-pooh the importance of the 'neutral' rate? What determines the *level* of the neutral rate? The propensity to save and the prospective marginal productivity of capital. But these are the determinants of the equilibrium rate of interest in classical economics. The 'neutral' rate puts his system within the schema of traditional political economy. He was rather naughty in wanting to seem more of a revolutionary than he really was. In this field his masterly contribution was his analysis of the forces governing the *market* rate of interest. But his most fundamental contribution in his whole work was his demonstration that there could be equilibrium with substantial unemployment, and that a downward revision of wages would not serve to cure that. Some commentators have suggested that Keynes's system depends on wages being inflexible downwards, as indeed they usually are in these days. This shows a complete lack of intellectual grasp of his system. His theory of equilibrium with unemployment in no wise depends on wages being inflexible downwards.

Why is there a liquidity preference? Some who have cash in hand may need to use it at dates and in amounts that are not at present quite certain. If they invest it in securities, they may be caught short by a fall in the value of the securities, i.e. a rise of interest rates, just when they want to use the money. If they are to be persuaded to buy securities, they must be paid some interest as an inducement to incur the risk. So interest has to be paid because there is uncertainty about the future rate of interest. I will quote here from my original book.[2]

Criticisms have been made of this theory on the ground that it leaves interest suspended, so to speak, in a void, there being interest because there is interest. Professor Robertson's subtle

---

[1] *The General Theory of Employment, Interest and Money*, pp. 242–3.
[2] *Towards a Dynamic Economics* (Macmillan, 1948) pp. 65–7.

thoughts on economics have for long solaced the hearts of economists, and great weight is due to any criticism he makes. I quote from page 25 of his *Essays in Monetary Theory*:

> Thus the rate of interest is what it is because it is expected to become other than it is; if it is not expected to become other than it is there is nothing left to tell us why it is what it is. The organ which secretes it has been amputated, and yet it still somehow exists – 'a grin without a cat'. Mr Plumptre of Toronto, in an unpublished paper, has aptly compared the position of the lenders of money under this theory with that of an insurance company which charges its clients a premium, the only risk against which it insures them being the risk that its premium will be raised. If we ask what ultimately governs the judgments of wealth owners as to why the rate of interest should be different in the future from what it is today, we are surely led straight back to the fundamental phenomena of productivity and thrift.

Or again, Mr Hicks writes: 'But to say that the rate of interest on perfectly safe securities is determined by nothing else but uncertainty of future interest rates seems to leave interest hanging by its own boot straps; one feels an obstinate conviction that there must be more in it than that.' Mr Hicks, however, does not base himself upon productivity and thrift but upon the cost incurred by the marginal transfer of money into short-dated securities, long-term interest being on this view ultimately governed by short-term interest.

These criticisms suggest that the Keynes theory of interest is circular; there is interest because the rate of interest is expected to change; in fine, there is interest, because there is expected to be interest. But why is there expected to be interest?

I do not think that this criticism is decisive. Surely there are some phenomena of the mind – and interest is nothing but a phenomenon of the mind, the resultant of thoughts and opinions, hopes and fears, itself only a promise, finally indeed an act, but one solely originating in the will of the parties, not a physical phenomenon at all – surely there are mental phenomena to which the dictum may correctly be applied that there is nothing true but thinking makes it so.

And I am inclined to think that this account of interest hanging by its own boot straps is an exaggeration. Consider a security with a certain par value due in twenty years, carrying 2½ per cent. Without interest the present value of £100 of such stock would be £150. This is a definite sum of money. But the market does not value the stock at £150, but at some lower figure, say, £100, to allow for the fact that the holder cannot be sure of getting the exact calculated sum, whatever it may be, between £150 and £100, at a date of his own choosing in the next twenty years. But, it will be objected that if there is no interest, and it is known that there will not in any case be any interest, will he not have a certainty of getting this appropriate sum? But this assumption is too far-reaching. In fairness to Keynes, I do not think we are entitled to assume, in rebutting the theory of liquidity preference, a world in which it was known that there never could be any interest, presumably a world in which there never had been any interest! And are not the critics going a little far? Did Keynes anywhere say that liquidity preference was the sole and only reason why there ever had been or could be interest? Or did he not rather merely say that liquidity preference was the sole determinant of the level of the current market rate of interest?

I am not prepared to reject Keynes's theory, even in the stripped form in which his critics present it, as untenable. It is certainly much more realistic than the other two possible theories that I have touched on. On the other hand I do not think that Keynes compels us to suppose that the market in brooding upon future prices, and on the uncertainties thereof, pays no regard whatever to Professor Robertson's 'productivity and thrift'.

In this passage I was much too weak in my defence of Keynes. I may have been *ébloui* by his pugnacious attitude to the classical doctrine, and have thought that he had departed further than he actually had. In the earlier work the 'natural' rate of interest is that which brings saving into equality with investment; this is classical doctrine. In the later work saving is *de facto* equal to investment, there are numerous natural rates conjugated with various levels of unemployment and a unique neutral rate. It is the market rate that is governed by what people think that the future rate of interest will be. If there were not underlying forces of productivity and thrift, the market would doubtless conclude that there would never be any positive rate of interest. I am confident that Keynes would have agreed with this.

It is right to add that Keynes held that, in times of deep depression and surplus unused productive capacity, no rate of interest, however low, would serve to bring the economy to full employment. The 'neutral' rate evaporated or, rather, assumed a high negative value; but the actual interest rate cannot have a negative value. Money supply policy would have to be supplemented by Public Works – more broadly, 'fiscal policy' – if full employment were to be secured.

Keynes's system is one of macro-statics. It is time to go over to dynamics.

The rate of interest may affect the values of both s_d and C_r, and, consequently the warranted growth rate. Its effect on s_d is, as has already been explained, uncertain. Do people save more or less when the rate of interest is high? A high saving ratio is conjugated with a high warranted growth rate. I assume that we are dealing with a moderate range of interest rates, such as prevails in fairly advanced countries, and not with rates of the order of 50 per cent. The effect of the rate on C_r is unequivocal. A low rate will tend to cause more capital intensive methods of production and, *pro tanto*, will be associated with a lower warranted growth rate. More of the available saving is taken up with financing more capitalistic methods and less accordingly left over for growth as such. While the interest rate is in principle a determinant of C_r, I have always stressed that in my own judgement, as a practical matter, it has a minimal influence on the capital-intensity of methods of production chosen. There are so many much more important factors, such as the availability of sufficient cadres of technologists, engineers, etc. A more capital-intensive method of production may require a larger supporting force of highly qualified people; or it could, in cases, be the other way round. Very important are the relative prices of the inputs other than capital disposal. We have already seen that it was the high price of human labour relatively to the prices of coal and other materials that caused the great increase of capital intensity in the U.S.A. in the late nineteenth century, although interest rates were running at a higher level than in the U.K.

Thus in practice the effect of the interest rate on saving – but we are fairly ignorant about what this is – might have a more significant influence on the warranted growth rate than its effect on the capital intensity of productive methods.

The next question that arises is whether we can frame a concept of a warranted rate of interest, to be conjugated with the warranted growth rate. Since the rate of interest is a determinant of s_d and C_r, although perhaps one of quite minor importance, the fundamental equation is not logically complete unless something can be said about the level of a normal interest rate appropriate to the warranted growth rate. It is assumed that, when there is an upward or downward departure from the (unstable) equilibrium of steady growth, monetary policy will be used to check these movements, establishing a supernormal rate to restrain a boom and a subnormal rate to correct a recession. But what should the rate be when all is in fact going forward steadily?

I have not been able to frame a satisfactory concept. In the long run this may not greatly matter, whether I am right or wrong in holding that the rate of interest does not have an important influence on s_d and C_r. Opinion in most countries is moving away from the ideal of *laissez-faire* capitalism, to which the concept of a warranted growth relates. There are two stages in this. It is now almost universally agreed that deliberate monetary policy, and, perhaps, also fiscal policy, should be used to check runaway movements away from an equilibrium, i.e. to control the business cycle. But opinion is now going further than this. It is coming to be held in wider circles that monetary and fiscal policies should be used to reduce unemployment (Keynesian macro-statics) and to ensure growth more nearly in accordance with the potential of the economy (growth theory). It may be too much to hope that the target of securing 'natural' growth, as I have defined it, will be achieved in the near future. But there will be attempts in that direction. Then what becomes all important is to determine what rate of interest is conjugated with natural growth; I call this the optimum rate of interest. Here the going is much easier. I shall discuss it later in this chapter.

An idea that occurred to me in seeking for a concept for warranted interest was that it should be that which would obtain, if the monetary authorities increased the money supply at the same rate as that at which the national income was growing. The amount of money would be needed to grow to finance a larger put through of goods and at the same time to increase the pool of liquidity, as required by the precautionary motive. This pool would presumably also grow, in the absence of special reasons to the contrary, at the same rate as national income. It might, of course, grow at a greater rate, if uncertainties were increasing, e.g. because rich people growing richer are more volatile in their incremental expenditures than poor people growing a little less poor. But I am not fully content with this attempt at a definition.

It is now needful to make a somewhat lengthy digression. It is with diffidence that I put myself into opposition to a view that has been extremely widely held recently, and also has respectable origins. The view is that, if there is a firm expectation of inflation, this expected increase of prices is reflected in the current rate of interest. Thus, if the interest rate on bonds would have been 3 per cent in the absence of the expectation of inflation, and if it is firmly believed that there will be a price increase of 3 per cent p.a. within the relevant time-horizon, the actual rate will stand at 6 per cent p.a. This view was held by the distinguished economist Alfred Marshall and referred to in his evidence on bi-metallism and the rupee, and propounded with his customary vigour by Irving Fisher, whose excellent doctrine about interest and the diminishing utility of income has already been referred to. Recent events have seemed to confirm the theory, with interest rates soaring to levels to find a precedent for which one would have to go back to the Middle Ages, and with inflation rampant. Holders of this view may, or ought to have been, a little disconcerted by the substantial fall of interest rates in most countries in 1970 and early 1971, when price inflation was on a plateau in some countries and still climbing in others, and the pessimistic view that high price inflation was likely to be endemic was growing stronger. (This was before the stance taken by the British Chancellor on 19 July 1971 and by the American President on 15 August, both promising more manful and vigorous measures to combat inflation.)

Keynes did not accept the view that the prosect of rising prices would raise the market rate of interest. In this I agree with him.

The point is that cash and bonds are both denominated in money. The rate of interest on bonds is the cost of going out of bonds into money, or, to put it the other way, it is the premium one receives if one goes out of money into bonds. It is, so to speak, the rate at which money exchanges for bonds. Since *neither* of these assets contains a hedge against inflation, it is not logical to affirm that the emergence of a sure prospect of inflation can alter the rate at which they exchange with each other. What is not logical cannot be accepted into the corpus of economic theory.

What the emergence of a sure prospect of inflation can do is to alter the relative valuation of those assets like bonds that have no hedge against and those that do, such as equities and real estate. And, sure enough, during the sixties the yield on equities dropped relatively to the yield on bonds both in the U.K. and the U.S.A.; indeed in both countries the yield on a fair sample of equities for the first time dropped below that on Government bonds. Meanwhile the values of various kinds of durable *objets d'art*, which also have a hedge against inflation, went soaring.

It has been objected that the yield on bonds, as determined by liquidity preference and the quantity of money outside the transactions circuit, may not be high enough to give a margin between their yield and the yield on equities equal to the prospective rate of inflation. The yield on equities cannot fall below zero or even to zero. So if one cannot get a sufficient spread between the yield on equities and that on bonds by the fall in the yield on equities, that on bonds must rise.

It must be noted, however, that, although one may speak of a certain prospect of inflation, there can never be absolute certainty. Let us suppose just a slight waver downwards in the rate of inflation, or merely in the expectation about prospective inflation. If this happened, it could cause a downward movement in the capital values of equities. Some investors in any kind of securities may desire to realise in due course; that is the object of having a capital market. If it so happens that an investor has need to realise at the time of the downward slither, he will make a capital loss. The net yield to him of the equity securities in question will have been the dividends that he has received minus the capital loss on sale. If the prices of the equities are standing at a high level at the time of purchase, the downward slither may not cause a greater proportionate loss than if they had been standing at a lower level; but the absolute loss will be greater, and it is the absolute loss that has to be subtracted from the dividends received, to determine the net yield – presumably negative – of the equities to the investor.

Now the representative investor may judge that there is only a small chance of such a downward slither. Then one should apply a very small probability fraction in assessing the amount of loss, should a downward slither occur. Of course in principle one would have to calculate for a range of downward slithers of various sizes. It may be argued that there is an equal probability of an unexpected upward slither. But, as is well known in actuarial matters, a 5 per cent chance of a loss of, say, £100,000 is not fully offset by a 5 per cent chance of a gain of £100,000.

Of course bonds may bump up and down for quite different reasons. But, if their yield has been higher, the net loss on the occasion of an equi-proportionate downward bump will be lower.

Accordingly I suggest that there is some yield above zero (price less than infinite) that enables equities to be a sufficient hedge for expectations of inflation within reasonable limits.

It is represented that on occasions of great inflation, like that of the Reichsmark in 1923, interest rates on bonds have risen to fantastic heights, like 50 per cent. Argue it as one may, it is futile to try to claim that such rates had nothing to do with inflation. I submit that on occasions of great inflation, the position is somewhat different. People are no longer comparing the merits of cash and bonds. The value of the total cash in the economy plummets; to all intents and purposes people cease holding cash, except for their barest immediate needs. It ceases to be thought of as one of two kinds of money-denomin-ated assets. I recall long queues of Germans in my bank in Berlin waiting to use their weekly pay to buy some securities, although they fully intended in the next week to sell them in order to do their shopping. My landlady, who had some cash in hand, but wanted to save herself the bother of going round to the bank, while I wanted to shop, offered to buy my paperback edition of Hobbes's *Leviathan*. She was not at all a philosophical lady.

The idea that an expected rate of inflation is impounded into the current rate of interest is, in my opinion, unacceptable. But I should like to suggest a compromise position as regards the relation of inflation to the rate of interest. The commonly held view is that it is the certainty, or strongly held belief, that inflation will proceed at a certain rate that is reflected into the interest rate. I suggest, on the contrary, that it is *uncertainty* about what may happen as regards inflation that can affect the interest rate.

If there is certainty or a strong belief that inflation will proceed, there will be persistent bidding for assets with a hedge against inflation and their prices will go up. The prospect of inflation may at a given point of time add to such assets, by stimulating real capital formation. It may also cause fraudulent people to produce a substantial quantity of sham *objets d'art*. But in relation to the total stock of real capital, its increase will be on the small side. Accordingly the increase of supply of assets containing a hedge against inflation owing to an inception of fresh fears about inflation, will be rather small; the elasticity of supply of such assets will be low. Thus, on the occasion of an inflection of the curve of anticipated inflation, supply and demand will be balanced mainly by a rise in the prices of assets or durable objects containing a hedge against inflation.

Investors will judge how far they want to go in sacrificing present income, in order to provide themselves with a hedge against inflation. That decision having been taken, they will have a residue to be divided between the two kinds of money-denominated assets, bonds and cash. The decision about how to divide these assets will be taken on standard Keynesian principles of liquidity preference. The decision having been taken about how much present income to sacrifice, owing to the sure, or almost sure, prospect of a given rate of inflation, the further decision as to how to divide money-denominated assets between bonds and cash will be determined in the following way. There is nothing in the certain prospect of inflation – we may substitute 'certain prospect of' for 'confident belief in' for the sake of simplicity – to influence this further division among money-denominated assets.

But let *uncertainty* about the future course of inflation increase. This may be a motive for an investor to keep liquid. His 'liquidity preference' schedule, i.e. his preference for cash, as against bonds, may rise. On the basis of a prospect of inflation of uncertain amount, he will have decided to sacrifice income by buying securities, real estate, etc., as a hedge against it. But he may have it in mind that he has not gone far enough in this sacrifice, or, alternatively, that he may have gone needlessly far. When there is substantial uncertainty, he will have it in mind that within six months or a year the inflation prospect may well have deteriorated or improved. So he may decide to keep more liquid, in order, if the new situation suggests it, to be able to go more deeply into low-yielding (or non-yielding) assets having a hedge against inflation. This will increase his demand for cash. The ratio of bonds to cash in the whole economy will not be affected by the representative investor's increased preference for cash, unless the central bank takes special measures to adapt the ratio. Consequently the increased preference for cash will cause the prices of bonds to fall, i.e. will cause the rate of interest to rise. This is in line with Keynes's 'liquidity preference' theory of the market rate of interest, but adds a new dimension to it.

It is to be stressed that this view, that *uncertainty* about the degree of prospective inflation tends to raise the rate of interest, is entirely different from the crude view that a sure, or near sure, prospect of inflation increases the current rate of interest by that amount.

In my judgement this crude idea that a sure (or near sure) prospect of future inflation is just written into the current rate of interest has done harm. Recently interest rates have been quite abnormally high, and this has probably injured world progress. (More recently they have dropped, but seem to be rising again.) When someone has urged that these high rates should be reduced, the relevant authorities tended to reply that it was impossible for them to bring this about, since the high rates were due to the sure prospect of inflation, and, whatever they did about the money supply, market rates of interest would continue to be high because of expected inflation. This is a fallacy.

If the high interest rates are due to increased liquidity preference (Keynes), owing to *uncertainties* about the future course of inflation, they can be reduced by the authorities increasing liquidity (Keynes).

The level of interest rates is, to some extent, an international phenomenon. In my judgement, the high world level of interest rates that has been prevailing has been due to the increasing shortage of world reserves in ratio to international transactions. This can be remedied only by concerted action to check the downslide of world reserves. But the authorities in each particular country could contribute something by causing its own level of interest rates to edge downwards as against the world average. At this point the national authorities object that they cannot cause their own interest rates to edge downwards, because these rates are governed by the prospective rate of inflation in their own countries. The determinants of the rates of domestic inflation will be discussed in the next chapter. It is the plea that nothing can be done to reduce domestic interest rates, because of the rate of inflation proceeding in each country, that has been doing great harm. At this point the digression ends.

Finally, it remains to consider the optimal rate of interest, as conjugated with the natural growth rate. We have to return to the central concept of the diminishing marginal utility of a pound, when income is rising. We have seen that there are two elements in the 'time preference', which is the fundamental reason why interest exists at all: lack of telescopic faculty and the diminishing marginal utility of income. The former of these must be left out of account when we are considering an optimum. Here we are concerned with something hortative. It has been the tradition of economics that its practitioners should analyse how things work out in fact and *also* assess the extent to which the way they do work out is conducive to the greatest happiness that can be yielded by our economic resources. Traditionally for instance, although not necessarily rightly, monopoly has been deemed to cause a discord between what actually happens and the best that could happen.

As judge and mentor, the economist must not assess a unit of happiness accruing in September 1971 as superior to a unit of happiness, of equal degree – subject to difficulties of measurement – accruing in September 1972. It is for him to be aloof and Olympian as between one year and another. Of course he is subject, in his prescriptions, to uncertainty about the degree of happiness that will be yielded by an event at a time removed from his own. He can know little about the shape of things to come or what will make human beings happy in A.D. 2071. Nonetheless he should eschew any systematic psychological preference. Uncertainty about the future may justify him in discounting projects for future benefit by a risk element. But this is different from a systematic time preference, by which individuals attach more importance to a Christmas pudding now than to the same one next year. Of course he must discount future benefits by reference to the decreasing marginal utilities of incomes, when incomes are rising.

The fundamental equation for the optimal interest rate is

$$\sigma = \frac{pc(\mathrm{G}n(\mathrm{con}))}{e} \quad \ldots\ldots\ldots\ldots\ldots \quad (1)$$

σ is the optimal rate of interest. $pc(\mathrm{G}n(\mathrm{con}))$ is the per caput natural (optimum) growth rate and e is the elasticity of the marginal diminishing utility of income schedule. $pc(\mathrm{G}n(\mathrm{con}))$ is in some degree determined by the rate of interest, so that simultaneous equations are involved.

It is important to state at once that this rate of interest is taken to be the rate that should be used in the choice between methods of varying degrees of capital intensity for producing a given commodity or service. In the schema of the natural growth rate, that is really its *sole* function. The saving ratio is the determinand, namely that which is required to implement growth at its natural rate; this ratio is independent of the propensity of individuals to save and consequently of the rate of interest, except to the extent that capital requirements (C_r) are dependent on that rate.

What determines the degree of capital intensity in the method of production chosen, among the various methods available, may be called the 'minimum acceptable rate of return on capital'. If this were zero, then, in choosing the method of production, we should simply take the one that showed the lowest total value of all kinds of input, *other* than waiting, as required per unit of output. But if some substantial sum has to be debited on account of inputs of waiting, that may twist the choice away from the more capital intensive methods.

The 'minimum acceptable rate of return on capital' in advanced societies appears to be considerably above the market rate of interest on first-class securities. This may be partly on account of risk. It is one thing to buy a security that can be sold, admittedly perhaps at a loss, in a capital market, and another to embody capital disposal in a specific type of plant, which can be redeemed only when that plant sweats out its output over a term of years. There may be other reasons. A firm may be unwilling to have too much of its capital in the hands of bond or share holders. It may also carry this idea into the future, when it may foresee that there will be opportunities for real capital extension more remunerative than any now available; if it goes up to the desirable limit in depending on outside capital now, it might have the choice in future of either going beyond that limit or of foregoing opportunities for extension that would be more remunerative than any now available. Again firms may be held back from paying projects by the maximum rate at which managerial personnel, well qualified to handle the specific problems, can be built up.

If one put $pcGn(\text{con})$ at 5 per cent p.a. and e at $\frac{1}{2}$,[1] both plausible figures, that would give a minimum acceptable rate of return on capital of 10 per cent p.a. This is well below the rates commonly prevailing, which may suggest that the methods of production in capitalist societies are usually not capital-intensive enough.

I have the impression that the minimum acceptable rate of return under capitalism is somewhat insensitive to moderate changes in the market rate of interest and to all short period changes. Firms have their regular methods of assessing prospective costs, including a standard rate of mark-up for profit. Their cost accountants do not hang over the telephone to get the latest news of interest rate changes; this is a further reason for holding that these interest rate changes may not have a substantial influence on the method of production chosen under capitalism. Monetary policy, which I believe to be very potent, works in quite a different manner. Easy money causes some firms to go forward with capital projects, the return on which

[1] See my reference to the results of two separate econometric investigations by Dr A. P. Barton and Dr Leif Johannson, yielding for ε the values of 0·5 and 0·53 respectively (*Economic Journal*, September 1963, p. 408).

would anyhow have been quite acceptable, but from which they have been held back by lack of available finance.

It may well be, however, that the large and rather long lasting increase of interest rates in recent years has caused many firms to raise their standard rates of mark-up, when costing, i.e. their 'minimum acceptable rate of return on capital' invested. This would tend to reduce the capital intensity adopted for fresh projects, and also, indeed, for replacements to worn-out capital.

I define elasticity (ε) in the manner of Alfred Marshall rather than by its converse as used by some more recent writers:

$$\varepsilon = \frac{\Delta\gamma}{\gamma} \div -\frac{\Delta u}{u}$$

where u stands for the marginal utility of income, which goes down as income rises. Thus if a 1 per cent increase of income causes a 2 per cent decline in marginal utility,

$$\frac{\Delta\gamma}{\gamma} \div -\frac{\Delta u}{u} = \frac{1}{100} \div -\frac{-2}{100} = \frac{1.}{2}$$

ε is the elasticity of a community utility function. This is a notion somewhat alien to traditional economics. However, community indifference curves have been finding their way into the theory of international trade.

Every individual has his own marginal utility of income function. Assessment of those of the separate citizens would be beyond computation. But there are likely to be significant differences, assessable (subject to wide margins of error), between the utility functions of those in different income brackets. The community utility function would be an average of the functions of each bracket, weighted, not by the total of income in each bracket, but by the number of heads in each bracket.

One might introduce a further complication: if the number of heads per income earner were significantly different in the different income brackets, a cross-section analysis would then be desirable. In the old days this would have sounded formidable, but with computer-assisted methods of calculation it should not be so. In former times – anyhow in the nineteenth century – it was the poor who had larger families, but this has been rapidly changing. In big families ε is presumably larger than in small ones.

The concept of ε implies cardinal measurement of utility. F. Y. Edgeworth, to whom, as inventor of the indifference curve, Pareto expressed indebtedness, was firmly of the belief that, in matters relating to utility, cardinal measurement would always continue to be indispensable. Indeed, he poured scorn on the contrary idea. The historic origin of the felt need for an indifference curve was that the demand curve uses money as a measure of utility, and any 'measure' should have a constant quantity of the thing that it measures. But any exchange transaction itself alters the marginal utility of money, so that money does not retain constancy of utility. (For small transactions, however, the alteration in its utility is negligible.) But in measuring income, we are not involved in an exchange. Indeed, money can be left out of it. We can measure income in terms of basketsful of commodities, properly weighted. One of the greatest economists of a later generation, Dr Ragnar Frisch, agrees with me that we have to retain cardinal measurement of utility.

We must proceed to the simultaneous equations. The need for them arises because the value of the expression on the right-hand side of equation 1 depends, even if possibly only to a very small degree, on the value of r_o. r stands for interest rate.

If the number of consumers rises at the same rate as that of producers, then, *ceteris paribus*, $pcGn(\text{con}) = Gn(\text{con})$. But it may not do so, owing a changing age distribution and a changing participation rate. The relation between the two can be expressed as

$$pcGn(\text{con}) = f(Gn(\text{con})) \quad \dots \dots \dots \quad (2)$$

If s_σ retains a constant value through time, $G(\text{con})n = Gn$. But it will not do so, unless technological progress is neutral. So we need an equation to express this:

$$G(\text{con})n = \phi(Gn) \quad \dots \dots \dots \dots \quad (3)$$

Technological progress has been defined as one that leaves the capital-output ratio (C_r) unchanged, at a given rate of interest. But at what rate of interest? For realism in this analysis the 'rate of interest' must be interpreted as referring to the minimum acceptable return on capital (MARC). And so we have

$$Gn\left(= \frac{s_\sigma}{C_r} \right) = \psi(r_\sigma) \quad \ldots\ldots\ldots\ldots \quad (4)$$

Thus we have four equations for four unknowns, namely r_σ, $pcGn(\text{con})$, $Gn(\text{con})$ and Gn.

Finally I may add that this somewhat complicated set-up, as required to determine the optimum rate of interest does not strike me as very important, since I do not believe that the rate of interest, anyhow within the limits normally prevailing in advanced societies, has much effect on the capital intensity of the methods of production chosen. Our economies would do well enough on a common sense evaluation of the minimum acceptable rate of return on capital of, say, 10 per cent, well below those currently prevailing, based on an estimate of potential growth of 5 per cent (on the low side) and an elasticity of the income utility schedule of $\frac{1}{2}$.

6 Inflation

The word 'inflation' is used in different senses, which, however, are related to each other. This may be bad for communication and even for thinking. A reader or listener may assume that a writer or speaker is using it in one sense when in fact he intends another. Worse, its user himself may not know what he does mean. Time and again, especially recently, when this word has been employed, I have been quite confident that its user could not stand up to an examination on what he thought that he meant by it. The harm may go further still and cause confusion in policy-making itself. It would probably be a good thing if its use was strictly outlawed, if only that were possible.

It is a fairly new word. It is not to be found in nineteenth-century dictionaries, except in the sense of blowing up a balloon. In those days they had to make do with such terms as debasement or depreciation of the currency.

The original sense probably combines inseparably the ideas of monetary and fiscal official policies. The government was said to inflate when it spent more than its income and financed its deficit by printing notes, or, in our modern sophisticated world, by borrowing from the central bank, or, possibly from commercial banks. Classic cases of inflation were the issue of *assignats* by the French revolutionary government of 1789 and the issue of notes in the American Civil War. At an earlier date (1717) there was the note issue by the French, under the advice of John Law, to finance various projects.

Historically, a country's currency was supposed to consist of, or to be convertible into, a certain weight of precious metal, and even after the Second World War currencies of countries held by the monetary authorities of other countries were thus convertible – whether this system has permanently broken down is not yet known (September 1971). Did the idea of 'inflation' entail that the issue of notes, etc. had been carried so far that convertibility had to be suspended? I believe so. It was certainly so in the French and American cases cited. This is a matter requiring detailed linguistic research. It was generally recognised that the sudden upsurge of government expenditures in major wars, combined with the technical difficulties in getting parallel tax increases, would necessitate 'inflation'.

In those connections the word was used both in active and in passive senses. It might be used for the actions of the naughty governments in issuing an excessive quantity of notes, etc., or for the state of affairs that resulted from that, namely the consequent rise of prices as denominated in the national currency.

More recently the word has been applied to milder events. In this connection does it still have the double sense, relating both to what the authorities have done (active) and also to what is actually occurring (passive)? It seems that it does not always have this double sense. In the discussion of the relation of the rate of interest to expected inflation in the last chapter, it was used only in the passive sense of rising prices, whatever the cause might be. The word is now often used for any rise of prices whatsoever. Thus it is sometimes said that 'an inflation of 2 per cent is tolerable'.

After the gold and silver discoveries in the American continent in the sixteenth century, world prices rose considerably. A similar, although more moderate, phenomenon, occurred owing to gold discoveries in California and Australia in the 1840s. Would modern usage affirm that there was 'inflation' in those periods? If so, the word would not have a double (active and passive) sense. Governments were not responsible for the discoveries of the precious metals. It would surely not be said that the gold diggers were 'inflating' the currencies of the world.

There is an analogous contemporary problem. In parts of the 1969–71 period prices in the U.K. and U.S.A. rose at a rate unprecedented in peacetime. But the governments were not printing an abnormal quantity of notes, etc. nor borrowing in abnormal quantities. The price increases were due to the granting of excessive wage increases. Here again the word 'inflation' must be taken to be used in a passive sense only. Some might argue that the government had actuated inflation because it had not taken the steps needed to prevent the wage increases.

This is stretching the use of language beyond the limits of what can be tolerated. What could it have done to check the wage increases? 'Oh', some say, 'it should have deflated.' Here we reach the very pitch of mental confusion. One is reminded of Keynes's duck that dived down to the bottom of the pond and got entangled in the weeds. A large inflation in the passive sense (increase of prices) was occurring. Apparently the active counterpart of this phenomenon was that the authorities were not deflating – whatever that may mean. Presumably it means having tighter money or a larger budget surplus. But would such 'deflation' have checked the rampant inflation? It is by no means certain. What a terminological tangle! But it is worse than that. It is tangled thinking, leading to tangled policy.

Recently people have settled down into thinking that some degree of annual inflation, moderate, it is to be hoped, will continue to be with us as far as the eye can see. This is a rather lamentable defeatism. One might almost regard it as a symptom of decadence. It we take a backward look, we do not find that inflation was endemic in England. For nearly a century after the Restoration (1660) the general trend of prices was downward, subject to transitory wartime interruptions. In the later part of the eighteenth century there was a moderate upward movement, doubtless connected with wars, but at the time of the outbreak of the war against the French revolution, prices were still not far from the 1660 level. Then came the great inflation, including suspension of convertibility. After the war the downward movement, again subject to interruptions, was resumed, and by 1850 prices were below the pre-war level. There was a flattening out in the middle of the century, probably due to the Californian and Australian gold discoveries already mentioned, after which a strong downturn was resumed, bringing prices in 1896 way below their 1660 level. Then came the South African gold discoveries and in particular the invention of the cyanide process, and also the South African war. These events were accompanied and followed by an upward trend of prices. *But even in 1933 prices were not above the 1660 level.* Then between the two world wars, there was not complete recovery from the great inflation of the first, but prices were trending downwards.[1]

[1] For a graph of the history as set out in the text, see the excellent fig. 7 in *British Economic Growth* by Phyllis Deane and W. A. Cole.

Why is all to be changed now? Why do we have to live in a brave new world of continuing inflation?

Some of us have advocated a large immediate rise in the price of gold. Have we thereby joined the ranks of inflationists? It has been counter-argued that this rise would open up the prospect of successive increases in the price of gold in future and would thereby stimulate its hoarding. I have always stressed that a rise in the price of gold should be accompanied by a firm and authoritative statement, preferably by some international authority, like the International Monetary Fund, that it had no intention of sponsoring further increases in future, but that the rise was designed as a once-over adjustment to the depreciation in the commodity values of paper currencies during and after the Second World War. A trebling of the price of gold would put gold back into its natural relation to other commodities. It just is not feasible, and indeed in all the circumstances would not be desirable, to reduce the general level of commodity prices, as expressed, say, in the dollar, to their 1939 level.

It is those who argue that a change in the price of gold now implies the need for further successive changes in the future that are the real inflationists. The implication is that the currency prices of goods and services will continue up and up; consequently, if gold is to retain its normal relation to other goods, its price in terms of currencies would have to be moved up successively. If we could achieve stable prices for the general run of goods and services, then the price of gold could also stay put. It is of course possible that, owing to the limited quantity of mineral deposits and the increasing output of goods and services due to rising world population and productivity, the output of gold would not keep pace with that of other goods. In that case it would be desirable – and it will anyhow be desirable – to supplement, and in the end supplant, the use of gold by international paper money, such as the Special Drawing Rights. But it is idle to suppose that these can suddenly be increased in quantity right away by enough for us to be able to dispense with gold as a medium of reserve for international settlement. An increase in the price of gold would provide us with a bridge between now and the time, some decades hence, when we can rely exclusively on international paper money as the sole reserve for international settlements. This advocacy of an increase in the price of gold is not to be identified with acquiescence in continuing inflation; the increase would be a retro-active measure.

It has been indicated that from 1660 the pound sterling preserved its commodity value, subject to ups and downs, until 1913. Looking further back, we may judge the matter in relation to debasements of the coins of the realm in terms of the precious metals. Our pennies date back at least to King Offa of Mercia, about whom schoolboys are, or anyhow, used to be, taught.[1] Within a century 240 of these came to be called 'a pound'. William the Conquerer had a lump of metal in the Tower of London and ordained that the silver penny should be of such a weight that 240 of them weighed the same as his lump of metal (the 'tower pound', slightly different from a troy pound). What a beastly thing it is that some bureaucrats should have wantonly destroyed a national institution dating back, without intermission, for a thousand years or more of our history! There are not many things in daily use by every man that he can think of as having been handed straight down from William the Conqueror (or even King Offa). Surely daily reminders of history add something to the pleasure of life.

When I was at school I was taught that a duodecimal system of numbers would probably, before too long, replace our present decimal system. Two extra numerical signs would be required and one-nought (10) would stand for what we now call 12. The advantage would be that the new 10 would be divisible by four, instead of only by two, numbers. However, things have not gone that way.

Our 240 pennies to the pound were a mixture of decimal and duodecimal. We might have had a great reform, by which we had 12 (as we now call it) pennies, written 10 pence, to the shilling, which dates back to the sixteenth century, and 10 shillings to the pound, giving us 144 pennies (but written 100 pence) to the pound. That would indeed have made calculating very much easier.

After William the Conqueror there was no debasement at all for about two centuries. By the time of Henry VIII, a culprit, the content of the penny had fallen to about one-half. Not a bad record for some five centuries. Between the recoinage of Queen

[1] A. E. Feaveryear, *The Pound Sterling*, p. 6.

Elizabeth I and 1931 there was only a small fractional debasement, partly due to the transition from a silver to a gold standard.

Thus we have a splendid record of stable money throughout our period of civilised history, apart from intervals of serious war. After the wars there was recovery and prices resumed their downward trend. It is only since the Second World War that things have been otherwise. And not only that; there is the acquiescence in a continuance of inflation into an indefinite future. Have we gone flabby? Have two serious wars undermined our stamina? Of course the phenomenon of inflation has not been confined to Britain.

Keynes's principal equation in his *Treatise* does not represent a macro-static nor a dynamic equilibrium, but it has one cardinal merit. It shows by separate terms the contributions of a cost push and a demand pull to an increase of prices.

$$P = \frac{E}{O} + \frac{I' - S}{R}$$

P is the price level of liquid consumption goods, E the earnings of the community per unit of time, O total output in the same period, I' the cost of production of new investment, S quantity of saving, as defined in the *Treatise* manner, already explained, and R the volume of liquid consumption. There is some confusion of terminology in this set-up, but it need not concern us. The main point is the clear demarcation of the two separate forces bearing on the course of prices. This is lost sight of in the *General Theory* where 'wage units' are taken as the unit of measurement.

In this earlier *Treatise* version of Keynes's thinking demand pull arises from the inequality of saving, as specially defined, and investment. In the *General Theory* Keynes repudiated his special definition of saving and argued strongly that it was better in the basic theory not to have any special definition of saving by which it could be unequal to investment. He had become embroiled in controversies with D. H. Robertson and Dr Fritz von Hayek, who each had their different special definitions. Yet there is a felt need for some kind of concept of this sort. Some favour the *ex ante* concept of Gunnar Myrdal. In the dynamic theory of this volume an analogous distinction is that between S, actual saving, and S_d, desired saving. This seems preferable to the distinction between *ex ante* and *ex post*, because S and S_d both obtain simultaneously at a given point of time. What has happened in the past may often be irrelevant.

In the *General Theory* demand pull inflation arises from aggregate effective demand in real terms exceeding the supply potential of the economy. That may be a better approach than his earlier one. But in the later volume cost push, as a separate and independent factor operating on prices, which stands out so clearly in the *Treatise* equation, largely disappears from view. That, in my judgement, has had an unfortunate effect on some subsequent developments of theory, and on policy also.

It must not be inferred that Keynes in the *Treatise* was a keen exponent of the idea of an inflation originating in a wage push. Rather the contrary. The general tenor of his thinking was that inflations usually originate from a demand pull and that increases in E/O are caused by demand pulls. In their scramble for available labour during a demand pull phase, employers would become more permissive in handing out wage increases in excess of productivity increases. But the point is, that even if rises in E/O are caused by demand pull inflation, the effect of such rises is *additive*.

A demand pull may be measured in terms of existing prices, i.e. before the inflation takes effect, as the excess of aggregate demand over the supply potential of the economy. One may express this as a sum of money, say £2 billion, or as a percentage, say 5 per cent. At first this excess may lead to a depletion of stocks; but in due course these will be reconstituted. Sooner or later, prices on the overall average must rise by 5 per cent, if aggregate demand is to be brought into equality with supply.

Consumers will be compelled to revise their plans for purchasing, because they will just not have the money to maintain them when prices have risen. This flattening (or decline) of real consumer demand may lead to a downward revision of investment plans. Furthermore, in a boom the rise in demand may be stronger on the side of investment goods, leading to a greater upward pull of prices there, than in the consumer goods sector. A squeeze may cause those ordering investment goods to make their contribution to a reduction of aggregate demand to the level of the supply potential of the economy.

In the foregoing it has been assumed that the prices of consumer goods rise while consumer incomes do not. The consequent squeeze on consumers will contribute to equating aggregate demand to the supply potential of the economy. But, in this environment, consumer incomes will probably rise by more than productivity increases. If they do, the price inflation in the economy will be more than 5 per cent. If employees obtain rises in excess of their increase of productivity, sufficient fully to compensate them for the initial price inflation, prices will in due course rise on the overall average, by 10 per cent. The point is that, if, and for as long as, a demand pull obtains, prices have got to rise by more than E/O (Earnings, but including only normal profit, divided by output). However successful employees may be in pushing up E, demand pull will defeat them. Prices will rise more than E/O by 5 per cent, or whatever the percentage may be (= excess of *real* aggregate demand over supply potential). Recipients of the excess price increases will save the revenue thus accruing to them.

A rise in E/O may occur in the absence of any demand-pull inflation. This was rather grudgingly admitted by Keynes, but he did not appear to regard it as important or likely to occur often. We have had much experience of it in recent years. If such a rise in E/O occurs, this will lead to a rise in prices. We may then get into a phase of what it is convenient to call wage-price spiralling. At the next round of bargains or contracts, employees are likely to demand increases, not only in proportion to their current rise in productivity, if they are so modest, but also with an increment of increase to compensate for the price inflation that has occurred since the last round. But, as this will have been due to the rise of E/O at the last round, the attempt to compensate for the inflation since the last round will inevitably cause further inflation before the next round; and so on. And in due course there can be an acceleration. After inflation has been proceeding merrily for a time, the employees may begin to ask for additional increases, not only to cover the inflation that has occurred since the last round, but also to cover further price increases as expected as likely to occur before the next. Producers who fix prices join in this game. On a review of their own prices, they may set them so as to cover probable wage and salary increases that may occur before the next review. And so, the upward spiralling proceeds. Unless the authorities do something to get to grips with the matter, the spiralling may accelerate.

It is sometimes argued that, in the absence of demand pull, producers will be unable to put up prices. This is doubtless true in the case of primary products, which are marketed in conditions of perfect competition. But in developed countries the major part of the output of goods and services is not so marketed; there may be very active competition in many cases, without there being 'perfect' competition in the technical sense. The competitor has a double reason for pushing cost increases on into prices. First, he may find, on doing his costing, that, if he does not raise his prices, he will be running at a loss and accordingly will eventually have to pack up. Secondly, he will probably argue that his competitors, being in the same boat, will have to do the same, so that he will not lose out in competition with them. Those generalisations are naturally subject to exceptions in particular cases. It is true that there have from time to time been squeezes on profit during the course of spiralling. The normal cause of such a squeeze, however, is not wage-price spiralling, but demand deflation, a very different matter. Whatever may be happening about wage-price spiralling and however violent it may be, there is demand deflation if the fraction of their incomes that consumers like to spend and the fraction of the productive resources required for justifiable real capital formation do not add up to one. Failure to understand this simple proposition, which is one of the most fundamental of economic dynamics has been the cause of the (irrational) surprise of some when they see strong price inflation accompanied by serious unemployment.

It is argued by some that, even if there is no current demand pull, the spiralling must be due to a demand occurring some time back – two, three, four years? Why? It is true that a phase of demand pull may set a process of wage-price spiralling going. This is an important reason for the authorities to be very vigilant about demand pull, and to correct it promptly, as soon as they see symptoms of it. It is one thing to affirm, very reasonably, that a phase of demand pull may be what sets a given wage-price spiralling going. It is quite another thing to affirm that any wage-price spiralling *must* have such a cause. Economic theory gives no justification for such a generalisation.

When there is spiralling, one may look around for an earlier year of demand-pull inflation. If one looks far enough, one can usually find one. But in affirming causation, one must watch quantities.

It is often said that the recent (1971) strong wage-price spiralling in the U.S.A. was the effect of demand pull inflation caused by the Vietnam war. It is urged that taxation as required to finance it was not raised soon enough. At an earlier period there was a Korean war, when the demand pull was greater. Defence expenditure was at its peak in 1952. (The peak came after the war was over and was due to the alarm caused by it in the U.S.A., which had let its defence apparatus run right down after the Second World War.) In 1952 defence expenditure absorbed 13·3 per cent of G.N.P. In 1967, the peak connected with Vietnam, it absorbed only 9·1 per cent of G.N.P. The Federal deficit was 1·9 per cent of G.N.P. in 1953 (peak). In 1967 it was somewhat less at 1·7 per cent. In the four years following Korea consumer prices rose up by only 2·4 per cent. In the three and a half years following Vietnam they rose up by 18·5 per cent. If the recent vast wage price spiralling was due to a moderate, and considerably earlier, demand pull associated with Vietnam, why did none such occur after the larger demand pull of Korea?

The Federal Reserve policy should also be considered. In 1967 the system increased the money supply by 8 per cent after a restrictive year (1966) in which the increase had been 3·2 per cent only. In early 1968 its policy was strict; there had been prolonged Congressional delay in passing the surtax, which had been considered a desirable fiscal supplement to monetary restraint. When at length it was passed in mid-1968, the Federal Reserve, fearing that the surtax, which may by this time have been no longer necessary, would have too restrictive an effect, eased its monetary policy considerably; it may be held that it over-compensated for the restrictive surtax. It increased the money supply by the annual rate of 11 per cent in the second half of the year; but in 1968 as a whole the increase was only 6·7 per cent. There may have been particular phases open to criticism. But it cannot be argued that there were excesses of

comparable order of magnitude to the great increases in consumer prices that followed.

There was a similar absence of excess in monetary and fiscal
policies in the U.K. Indeed, in 1968 the British authorities
began building Budget surpluses of huge magnitude, quite
without precedent in the U.K. or any other country. The
banking policy was quite moderate. And yet the inflation of
wages and prices was very great and substantially larger than
that in the U.S.A.

Why then did these inflations occur? Events must have
causes. In my opinion these causes are not to be found among
factors to which the term economic can by usage be applied –
supply and demand pressures, relations of marginal productivity
to marginal utility, degree of monopoly, etc. Rather they should
be analysed with the aid of concepts belonging to a wider field
of sociology. There may occur a greater degree of activism on
the part of those asking for more pay. 'We are going to fight for
this; do not think that you can get away with it by a negative
attitude.' On the side of those who grant increases, there may be
more permissiveness. This is balanced by greater activism on
their part on the other side of the counter, a shameless putting
up of prices, in its turn confronted by greater permissiveness on
the part of the final buyers. In the old days there was often
sharp and angry protest by the customer, used to paying a
certain price for a certain object, if that price was raised. He
might withdraw his custom from the shop. Nowadays price
increases are accepted as part of the natural order of things
without much protest. 'We know that there is something called
"inflation" going on, and we have to accept this sort of thing.'
Anyhow, most of these customers are getting more pay themselves. And thus the vicious circle – vicious spiral – is completed.
Pensioners and others with fixed incomes are the victims and
their consequent suffering is often great. They may have to
abandon their planned way of life.

But still the basic cause eludes us. Why should important
sections of the population become more activist in a certain
period of history? I believe the cause to be due to the rising
real standard of living. There may be a crucial strand in the
upward-sloping shore, where earners are sufficiently raised
above subsistence living for their anxieties to drop. State

assistance in its various forms doubtless contributes to relief from anxiety.

One is reminded of the greatest sociologist of them all, de Tocqueville. For many years people believed that the French Revolution was the final flare up of the French population, progressively ground down in increasing poverty and misery, until they could bear it no longer. In his *L'Ancien Regime* de Tocqueville shows that the eighteenth century was for France a period of enlightenment and amelioration in many departments of human affairs. But there was a growing concentration of power in the hands of the not very efficient bureaucracy in Paris. Meanwhile the people were becoming more demanding; their horizons had widened; they had long since come out of the dark cave of abject poverty. So, not content with the improvements to date, they asked for more – that the nobility should take their share in the burden of taxation, that the people should be given effective representation in the legislative process. As the child comes to participate more fully in the amenities of the 'grown-ups', he 'asks for more'.

Doubtless the demands of the French revolutionaries, at least in the early stages, were more justified and capable of being granted without injury, than the demands of earners for excessive pay increases, which, if not partly balanced by an increase of prices, would before long reduce profit to zero and bring free enterprise economies to an end. The greater recent 'uppishness' in the inflationary sphere may be regarded as first cousin to other sociological manifestations, like student unrest, increasing violence and, in the U.S.A., racial troubles.

If it is true that the cause of the acceleration of wage and price increases has sociological roots of the kind described, then it is idle to hope to cure the evil by the traditional remedies of tight money or budget surplus. These are geared to eliminating demand inflation. It is doubtful if they are suitable for correcting such moderate wage-price spiralling as may simply be the aftermath of a demand inflation. This will be further discussed.

They are clearly entirely inappropriate for dealing with the much larger and disproportionate wage and price increases of the recent period. But this does not mean that we should passively acquiesce in the great evil. What is needed is a direct confrontation. 'We are just not going to allow you to destroy so much that is valuable in our society by your excessive activism.'

The method of direct confrontation is what is known as 'incomes policy', consisting in official interference with the course of wages and prices. The target, unhappily not likely to be achievable in the near future, but only within a year or two, should be an overall average increase of wages not greater than that of productivity, and stable prices. It is still not beyond the bounds of possibility that this could be achieved by voluntary methods, based on an agreement in principle by leading industrialists and trade unionists. Some two months after the victory of the British Labour Party in the General Election of 1964, Mr George Brown (now Lord George-Brown) thought that he had got an effective agreement and was photographed gaily holding up the relevant piece of paper. But in the event it proved not to be effective.

If effective voluntary agreement cannot be obtained, then methods with legal sanctions must be adopted. The evil is too great to be tolerated. That is surely the opinion of the democracy.

It seems that the Conservative Government of Britain (Mr Barber's statement on 19 July 1971) and the Republican Government of the U.S.A. (President Nixon's statement on 15 August 1971) are both now committed to an 'incomes policy', although both governments had previously been strongly opposed to one on doctrinal grounds.

Why is something so new now required? It is not unreasonable to expect, with progress, the need for novelties in economic policy, as in other spheres. The phenomenon of violent upsurges in prices and wages in peace time is new in industrial countries, and a new phenomenon may be expected to need some new method for coping with it. This is further enforced, if it is true that the new phenomenon has sociological causes outside the realm of economics, as we have hitherto understood it.

And is direct interference entirely new? For centuries in England maximum legal wages were fixed by the Justices of the Peace. Doubtless trade union leaders would not at present be disposed to hand the matter over to the J.P.s. So a new authority is required.

The text in the foregoing paragraphs has become somewhat hortatory. Is there any reason why economic dynamics should not occasionally, like traditional economics, take on a flavour of political economy?

The theoretical point is that there is nothing in dynamic theory, or in static theory either, that justifies the statement that wage or price inflation or wage-price spiralling *must* be caused by a simultaneous or preceding demand inflation (aggregate demand > the supply potential of the economy). It may be or it may not be. Empirical reasoning suggests that the recent wage and price inflation has not been so caused, because the quantities are wrong. In empirical reasoning one must always have regard to quantities.

On 18 July 1969, I wrote a letter to the *Economist* newspaper, on the matter of inflation, for which they provided a headline in the words 'Harrod's dichotomy'.

It has already been explained how overall excess demand almost inevitably causes an increase of prices. There is a gap to be filled. This is quite different from the proposition, widely taken as axiomatic for a good many years now, that rising aggregate demand tends to raise prices. This, in relation to the history of economic thought since Adam Smith, is a comparatively novel doctrine.

Traditional economics (apart from the period before 1850) consisted of what should now be called micro-statics. It was accordingly concerned with the determination of the prices of particular goods and services. When we pass over to macro-economics (static or dynamic) we are concerned with the general price level. It is to be stressed that this general price level is determined by the sum of individual prices. One cannot have the majority of the latter going up while the former goes down, or conversely. So we must examine the forces that govern the movement of particular prices. If an increase of demand does not tend on the overall average to raise the prices of each particular commodity, it cannot tend to raise the general price level.

Theory as regards particular prices used to be quite clear and regularly demonstrated on a blackboard to first-year classes in economics. An increase of demand would tend to raise prices in the case of commodities subject to diminishing returns and to reduce prices in the case of those subject to increasing returns. Thus, so far as the general price level is concerned, all depends on whether the commodities subject to diminishing returns do or do not outweigh those subject to increasing returns. The former consist primarily of food and raw materials and of those commodities in the cost of production of which raw materials have a heavy weight. In manufacture, and also in the growingly important sphere of services, increasing returns on the whole prevail.

In advanced countries food (diminishing returns) consumption grows less than total expenditure (in real terms). Furthermore, the raw material content of final products grows less, because with rising real income people tend towards using more of their incomes on the purchase of highly finished goods, in which the raw material content is lower. Thus in advanced countries one would expect the proportion of income devoted to the increasing returns sector to be higher than that devoted to the diminishing returns sector.

Furthermore, there are more apt to be world prices for goods in the diminishing returns sector, than in that of increasing returns, since the former are bought and sold in perfect markets. While there is some tendency for world competition in the sphere of finished products to grow, it remains lower than that for food and raw materials. There cannot be world competition for the services provided in each separate country, apart from tourism, and these services are tending to be a growing proportion of all goods and services purchased in advanced countries.

There is another point. The more subject a given article is to world pricing, the less effect will a given percentage increase in the demand for it in a particular country have on its price in that country. So, in considering the effect of an overall rise of demand in a particular country on the general level of prices in the country, one should give diminishing returns goods a lower weight than that which corresponds to their proportion of real national expenditure in that country.

Thus, by traditional economics, one would expect a rise in aggregate demand to cause a fall in the general price level in advanced countries, and conversely.

In relation to upward and downward movements in (real) aggregate demand, there are two quite separate forces at work, according to the circumstances, which are *different in kind*. This is of the essence of the 'Harrod dichotomy'. If the real demand for goods and services is above the supply potential of the economy, there is a gap that has to be filled. If it is not filled by rising prices, there must inevitably be a depletion of stocks. This depletion cannot go on indefinitely, so that, in due course, the gap will have to be filled by price inflation. But if aggregate real demand is below the supply potential of the economy, there is no necessity for prices to fall by enough to fill the gap. It can be filled by a corresponding fall of production and increase of unemployment. We have seen this happen often enough.

When aggregate real demand is above the supply potential of the economy, and price-inflation ensues by consequence, monetary and fiscal policies should be addressed to reducing aggregate real demand. There is an alternative here of logical necessity. Either the gap (aggregate real demand > supply potential) can be eliminated by monetary and fiscal policies, framed to reduce aggregate real demand to the supply potential, or it can be eliminated by the relevant amount of price inflation. There is no further alternative. But if aggregate real demand is below the supply potential, reducing aggregate real demand will have no necessary, or even probable, tendency to eliminate, or reduce any price inflation that may have been occurring. When aggregate real demand exceeds the supply potential there is a necessary tendency for prices to rise (demand pull inflation). But when aggregate real demand is below the supply potential, there is no necessary tendency for prices to fall. If a wages pull is proceeding, a price rise may continue unabated.

The fundamental difference between the two situations is that in the excess demand situation prices rise inevitably; the rise can be halted, or reduced, by monetary and fiscal measures that reduce aggregate real demand. But when demand is below the supply potential there is no necessary downward pull on prices; the gap between potential supply and demand may be filled, and obviously has been so filled on numerous occasions, by a fall in production and employment. Consequently, in this situation, monetary and fiscal policies may not, and usually do not, have the remedial effect that they have in the converse situation.

And they may have a perverse effect. If, on the overall average, the production of goods and services is subject to increasing returns to scale, monetary and fiscal policies designed to reduce demand will raise costs. In this area prices asked depend on costs, so that a reduction of aggregate demand is

likely to compel the suppliers of goods and services to raise
prices. Per contra, expansionist monetary and fiscal policies
would enable them to reduce prices. A reduction of prices
sounds a little unrealistic in relation to recent events, save for
exceptional cases like the reduction of air fares. But, if a wage
push is proceeding, a rise of demand may make it possible for
firms to absorb a greater part of the higher wages by a reduction
of unit costs than they otherwise could. A rise of demand would
in that case reduce the rate of price inflation. If, in these circumstances, the authorities use monetary and fiscal policies to cur-
tail aggregate demand, this will have the malign effect of
increasing price inflation.

It is argued that a reduction of aggregate demand, even
when that is below the supply potential of the economy, should
reduce price inflation by causing an abatement of the wage push,
on the lines of the Phillips curve, for which experience in the
U.K. does not in fact provide evidence. Two points must be
made. Even if rising unemployment caused an abatement of the
rate of wage increases, this might well reduce money costs less
than the fall of turnover increased real unit costs. In this case
deflation, so called, would have a price-inflationary effect.

The second point is that it need not be denied, that, if deflationary monetary and fiscal policies were carried to the point
of producing really massive unemployment, like that of 1931,
this might have a damping effect on the request for the granting
of higher wages. A crisis atmosphere is produced. Everyone has
to buckle to, and do his best in such circumstances; wage
claims will be abated. But the creation of such massive unemployment as that required to produce a 'crisis atmosphere'
should not be regarded as part of the normal machinery of
monetary and fiscal policies in the present age. A step forward
was taken in the Second World War in relation to the targets of
policy; it was decided that massive unemployment such as that
of the thirties should not be allowed to recur, and could be pre-
vented. We do not want to go back on that, nor shall.

The upshot is that a new weapon of policy is required, an
'incomes policy'.

Inflation is an evil. It may be due to aggregate demand being
currently in excess of the supply potential of the economy. This
possibility was implicitly recognised by writers on the business

cycle from the beginning; but it was first introduced into the corpus of basic formal economy theory by Keynes. He did not dilate on its consequences for economic policy, since for most of the period of his creative work in general theory, the world was plagued by a deficiency of aggregate demand and he addressed his constructive proposals mainly to that phase. He did, however, make practical suggestions in relation to excessive demand in the Second World War in his pamphlet on 'How to pay for the war'

There is no problem here. The remedy is to reduce aggregate demand by monetary and fiscal policies – reduce the money supply and increase the ratio of taxation to governmental expenditure.

If aggregate demand is running below the supply potential, so that there is underemployment of those at work and/or visible unemployment in addition to that due to regular frictional causes, the opposite remedies are appropriate – increase the money supply and reduce the ratio of taxation to governmental expenditure. This is quite independent of whether inflation is simultaneously proceeding. Unemployment and inflation are both evils; the former is the greater evil. It entails that persons who want to work cannot find jobs, which must be a source of distress to them, and that the community is needlessly deprived of an output of goods and services that could add to its happiness. Inflation causes many tiresome inconveniences and also important suffering to those with fixed incomes. A conscientious government could remedy the latter evil by the provision of compensatory allowances for the victims; but it would do better to stop the inflation.

If depressing demand, when it is already below the supply potential, is ruled out, no remedy has been advanced except an 'incomes policy', namely an arrangement by which on the overall average earnings do not go up by more than the overall average increase in productivity, and prices are accordingly held stable. This arrangement might be secured by continuing round-table negotiations. If that, after fair trial, proves impossible, resort must be had to legal enforcement.

It is objected that the equitable administration of such a law would need a bureaucracy of substantial size. That would be regrettable. But it is rather a perverse objection in an age when vast bureaucracies are being built up on all sides to achieve much less important objectives.

Some may criticise the formula on the ground that wages should be allowed to go up somewhat more than output per head, in order to secure a more equitable distribution of the national income. It is to be noted that salary earners, including those in upper income brackets, are in the inflation race and sometimes seem to be winning. There is a technical difficulty here. In a regime of stable prices earnings could be allowed to go up over a continuing period only by a small fraction of 1 per cent p.a. in excess of productivity, if profits were not to be eliminated altogether and the system of private enterprise terminated. To get a precise very small amount of increase of overall average earnings in excess of productivity would be a matter of great statistical and administrative difficulty. There may be errors in getting the overall average increase of earnings exactly equal to that of productivity. But this is a manageable target, and there can be *ex post* adjustments. It is generally agreed that a redistribution of incomes, if and when required to secure greater equity, should be achieved by adjustments in the scales of progressive taxation.

Finally, there is the question of the 'Harrod dichotomy'. It has been widely held that measures to increase real aggregate demand will always have a price inflationary effect. According to the 'dichotomy' such measures will have a price inflationary effect, only when real aggregate demand is currently running above, or at, or, perhaps one should cautiously add, almost at, the supply potential of the economy. If, on the other hand, it is running below the supply potential, expansionist measures will tend to reduce real costs and thereby raise productivity. Thus the increase of earnings allowable by the productivity criterion will be greater with an expansionist policy than it would otherwise be. Consequently an expansionist policy would ease the headaches of those who have to settle earning rates, whether at voluntary round-tables or in statutory committees.

The statements (already referred to) of Mr Barber and President Nixon imply that an expansionist policy will help, not hinder, the fight against inflation. I know of no official statements in this sense ever having been made before. If these statements are followed up by effective action, they could be a turning point in the history of economic policy.

7 Problems and Conflicts

Warranted and natural rates of growth are entirely different concepts, and they have different determinants. The warranted rate is that at which desired saving is equal to required investment. If one plotted various growth rates along the horizontal axis and desired saving and required investment on the vertical axis, one would get two upward-sloping curves with investment rising above saving at the point of intersection. The reason for this is that a substantial part of investment is a direct function of the growth rate, being needed to sustain increments of production, while saving is for the most part – we need not say entirely – a function of the whole of income. Thus the amount of investment required is more strongly affected by the size of the increments of income than the amount of desired saving. In the determination of the warranted rate the amount of saving that people want to make is, so to say, the lord and master.

The determinants of the natural rate are, by contrast, the increase in the population of working age and the nature of current technological progress. Saving is the servant.

Traditionally monetary and fiscal policies have been considered as correctives, to be used to check runaway movements of departure from the warranted rate. Such movements of departure, will, if unchecked, cause conditions of inflation (demand pull) or deflation. It is to be noted that demand pull inflation may occur before the ceiling of full employment is reached. If prices are inflexible downwards, deflation may simply take the form of rising unemployment. The question will be raised whether there are in fact, or ought to be, or can properly be, other functions for monetary and fiscal policies to perform. It may appear that the respective proper roles of monetary and fiscal policies should be more sharply distinguished than they usually have been. To date we still have references to a 'package deal' of monetary and fiscal measures designed to give a boost to the economy or damp it down.

Normally one would expect, and this was the older traditional doctrine (cf. Walter Bagehot), that policies designed to check runaway movements would do their work rather quickly. Recently there has been a tendency to keep expansionary or restrictive policies, especially the latter, in operation for rather long periods. This may be because the policy makers have in mind objectives other than simply checking runaway movements. For instance, deflationary policies may be continued with a view to preventing wage-price spiralling. They may continue to be pursued, even although it is obvious that they are causing an increase of unemployment. This is a highly undesirable use of these policies, and is little likely, in effect, to have any success in abating a wage-price spiralling. On the other side expansionist policies may be used prolongedly to raise employment. The appropriateness of this depends on whether the warranted growth rate is such as to entail a certain amount of unemployment. If it is, then the prolongation of the expansionist policy will entail price inflation. Then the authorities will start moving in the opposite direction. And thus we shall get irrational movements of a confused character. We shall continue in confusion until growth theory has progressed further and been able, in consequence, to formulate well based principles in applied economics that policy makers can understand and act upon.

A distinction was drawn between the 'normal' warranted growth that applies when the system is in equilibrium (unstable) and special warranted growth rates, that apply only in the course of runaways, when the system is not in equilibrium at all. The special and temporary warranted growth rate may chase the actual rate upwards or downwards. It was only by reference to this that we were able to explain how a recession might find a bottom, apart from policy measures deliberately designed to terminate it.

Monetary and fiscal policies are primarily designed to influence the actual rate by bringing it back into line with the normal warranted rate, and thus putting an end to processes of inflation and deflation. But if they are kept in being for a substantial time, – for other reasons – they could have an influence on the *normal* warranted growth rate itself. For instance, if a rate of interest, higher than people have previously been used to, is kept in being for a substantial period, people may begin to think of it as part of the normal furniture of life. 'This is the new world that we now have to live in.' Something of this sort appears to have happened in the 1960s. Or again, a government, having, in the first instance, taken a stricter view about its Budget deficit, in order to combat inflation, may by habit – whatever party is in power – become imbued with a more Gladstonian outlook.

This brings us to a central paradox. Measures calculated to influence actual growth upwards or downwards have the opposite effect, to the extent that they have any effect, on the normal warranted growth rate. Whether high interest has any effect on the personal saving ratio we have seen to be doubtful. It is commonly supposed that it tends to raise it. Any rise in the saving ratio raises the warranted growth rate, while, of course, tending to depress the actual one. If high interest has any effect on the capital intensity of methods of production, it will be to reduce it. This raises the warranted growth rate, while reducing the actual one. Tight money should in itself have more influence than the interest rate, as such, in reducing the capital intensity of methods of production chosen; this also raises the warranted growth rate, while reducing the actual one. On the fiscal side a shift towards reducing a budget surplus or increasing a deficit will assuredly reduce the warranted growth rate, while raising the actual one.

If continuing deflation tends to raise the warranted growth rate, it might be thought that this was a good thing. All depends on whether the previous warranted growth rate was above or below the natural rate. If it was above, the policy measures that raise it further are bad. The actual growth rate cannot be for the major part of the time above the natural rate. The latter imposes a limit. The actual rate can, of course, be above the natural rate during periods of recovery from an underemployment situation. Accordingly, if the warranted rate is above the natural rate, the actual rate must be below the warranted rate for the greater part of the time. During this time, there will be cumulative depressive forces in operation; the authorities may, rightly, think it their duty to adopt expansionist measures during such periods to hoist up the actual rate to the warranted rate. But, if the warranted rate is above the natural rate, the authorities cannot keep the actual rate at the warranted rate level for most of the time. There is just too much saving. This is the dynamised version of what was known among post-Keynesian writers as the 'stagnation thesis'. The phenomena pertaining to this thesis do not seem to have reared their ugly heads since the Second World War as much as the post-war proponents of it feared that they would. This may have been due to the vast post-war requirements for industrial reconstruction, to a much more permissive attitude in regard to these – largely influenced by Keynes himself – and some subsequent minor wars. Nonetheless, symptoms of stagnation began to appear in the late sixties, anyhow in the U.S.A. and U.K. So we must continue to keep a weather eye on the dynamised version of the stagnation thesis.

It may be useful to sort out the relation between the three growth rates in tabular form as shown on page 104.

The theory of permutations and combinations entails that there should be eight instances in this table. (The relation of actual to natural growth is purely fortuitous, so that there would be no point in including in the table alternatives in this regard.) The reason why there are only seven is that at full employment it is impossible for the actual growth rate to be above the natural growth rate. Out of the seven cases only in those of 1 and 3 is there no conflict. In the first case, actual growth is tending to fall below the full employment position and is below the warranted rate. The latter relation, if uncorrected, will entail cumulative recession, until some bottom is reached. The third case is similar, except that at the initial point there is already unemployment. Accordingly reflation is needed to check the recession and bring the actual rate up to the warranted level. Furthermore, to the extent that reflation has to be maintained for some time, it will have a good long run effect. It will tend to reduce the warranted growth rate towards the natural growth rate. As long as the warranted rate is above the natural rate, there will be endemic trouble.

The first three cases are all instances of the dynamised version of the 'stagnation thesis'. They show more saving than is required to sustain a growing work force and to implement technological innovations. It is required to reduce the quantity of saving. In cases 1 and 3, it cannot be assumed that reflation can be kept

Synopsis of disequilibria and of effects of expansionist policies on them.
Deflation would show opposite consequences. The symbol O *shows the full employment position.*

	Conflict or Harmony	1. Effect on full employment	2. Effect on inflationary or deflationary pressure	3. Effect on long-run growth equilibrum
1	Harmony	Good	Good	Good
2	Conflict	Good	Bad	Good
3	Harmony	Good	Good	Good
4	Conflict	Good	Bad	Bad
5	Conflict	Good	Good	Bad
6	Conflict	Good	Bad	Bad
7	Conflict	Good	Good	Bad

in being for long enough to reduce the normal warranted growth rate substantially without eventually causing inflationary pressure. Thus although there is no conflict at the moment, there is the potentiality of conflict.

In the second case conflict is already present. The economy has got the bit between its teeth and is moving out of recession. From one point of view, the more quickly the unemployed can be brought to work, the better. In the whole complex of considerations, unemployment is the greatest evil. A little reflation would speed up this salutary development still further. But if we reflate, or even adopt a neutral stance of *laissez-faire*, demand pull inflation will start. It is important to observe that demand pull inflation can occur when there is still substantial unemployment; there may not be enough saving to finance a recovery proceeding above a certain rate. Of course the situation may be mitigated if there is unused capacity left over from a previous slump; but there may not be, or not sufficient.

One idea would be to have a little deflation, not so much as to check recovery altogether, but enough to hold it down to the pace indicated by the warranted growth rate. This would be somewhat defeatist.

Then a further problem lies in store. Once full employment is reached, it is impossible for the economy to move forward at a greater rate than that shown by the natural rate curve. But this is below the warranted rate. Accordingly recession is inevitable, unless special measures are taken. Of course there are likely to be time-lags. The economy may bump along the top for a period. I have already repudiated the idea that I regard the instability principle as involving anything like a knife-edge (Chapter 3).

And now we come to the crux of the matter. The vital time to apply reflation in an economy of excess saving is when it has reached the limit of the boom and is on the full employment ceiling. Once it slips down from there, all the old problems will reappear. The Government should start running sufficient Budget deficits by reducing taxes to offset the excess savings by persons and companies. During the recovery the tendency towards excess savings is masked; the economy is advancing at above its natural rate with consequent supernormal investment requirements, which utilise the excess saving. But once full employment is reached, the economy cannot advance at above its natural rate, and consequently, investment requirements will fall below the level of those prevailing during recovery.

There is a paradox involved here, to which there may be mental resistance. The foot should be put on the accelerator when unemployment is at its minimum level. The view of the 'man-in-the-street' probably is that the foot should be put on the accelerator, when the economy is in recession and unemployment is increasing, a view that seems natural and plausible. But it is wrong. The foot should be put on the accelerator when unemployment is still at a minimum. Any delay will set up problems in store in the period ahead. It is this paradox that makes it so important for economic dynamics to establish, with the agreement of all respectable economists, its basic axioms, and for experts in applied economics to translate them, as and when they are established, into maxims of policy.

It was stated above that, when the economy is bumping along the ceiling of full employment, the Government ought to *reduce* taxation by a significant amount. At that point the introduction of additional public works (a reflationary measure) would be inappropriate, since, by hypothesis, the economy would be fully employed at that point. There would be no one to get to work on the newly instituted 'public works'.

While, and because, I entirely agree with Professor Kenneth Galbraith, as I have already indicated, that a greater proportion of resources, both in the U.K. and the U.S.A., should be devoted to public works – slum renewal, preservation of the countryside, etc., I do not regard the amount spent on public works as an appropriate regulator of the business cycle or of the actual growth rate. I have stated from my early days that this idea is impractical. Most public works entail planning over a substantial period of time; the relevant labour has to be mobilised, etc. It is not feasible to suspend work on projects, all in the midst, because the Treasury notifies that a deflationary policy has become the order of the day.

Public works should be taken out of the list of the available tools – presumably they already have been – for regulating the business cycle or maintaining optimum growth. I hold, in sympathy with Professor Kenneth Galbraith, that public works should come to constitute a growingly important element in the total national output. But that is not relevant to the subject of this chapter.

It is the fiscal weapon, notably tax reduction without any reduction of government expenditure, that appears to be the all-important one at the top of the boom. It has its crucial influence, when natural growth can no longer keep pace with warranted growth. It is the excess of normal warranted growth over natural growth that necessitates a recession when the economy is at its full employment ceiling; tax reduction can offset the excess and thereby enable full employment to be maintained. If the government reduces taxes by £1 million and thus reduces its saving (or increases its dis-saving) by that amount, the tax payer will doubtless save some part of his reduced tax liability, but not the whole of it. Thus there will be some net reduction of saving.

While some mental resistance to expansionist measures to increase demand at the top of the boom may be regarded as natural and healthy, although misguided, there may be another strand in the thinking on this subject that is entirely unhealthy. At the top of the boom wage-price spiralling may be rampaging. This is entirely irrelevant in relation to what ought to be done to regulate the growth of output. Wage-price spiralling may also, of course, rampage in periods of industrial recession or stagnation, as has been seen lately. But it may well have a stronger influence on policy makers at the top of the boom. 'It would be madness to take measures to increase demand, when unemployment is low, and inflation (wage-price spiralling) rampant.' This kind of thinking has also occurred in the international sphere, where there have been repeated negative expressions of opinion about increasing the at present woefully inadequate world reserves at a time when 'inflation' (in fact almost entirely cost-push inflation) was strong. 'Surely', it has been often said, 'it would be unwise to increase world reserves in the presence of nearly world-wide inflation.' The level of world reserves has presumably no relation to cost-push inflation in the different countries. A low level of these reserves may actually promote demand-pull inflation in some countries, by making them think it needful to increase barriers to imports, which have a local demand-pull inflationary effect.

To return to the domestic front, policy makers should clear

their minds of any idea that expanionist measures will have a price inflationary consequence, except when aggregate effective demand is equal to or above the supply potential of the economy. This proposition, stated earlier (the 'Harrod dichotomy'), in fact needs some modification. If demand is equal to the supply potential, positive expansionist measures may be needful to make it continue to increase, but only at a rate not greater than the natural growth rate of the economy.

The foregoing has suggested that in the case of excess-saving economies, it is needful to regulate the supply of saving (by reducing Budget surpluses or increasing Budget deficits) if these economies are to be kept expanding on an even keel. It is this thought that takes us over from the theory of *laissez-faire* capitalism, with its 'warranted' growth rate, to that of growth in accordance with what the advance of technology renders possible. What persons and companies choose to save ceases to be the determinant of growth; in its place we have an optimum rate of saving determined by the nature of current technological progress and associated with it a 'natural' (optimum) rate of growth. Once this is appreciated, it is seen to be the demise of old-fashioned *laissez-faire* economics (and 'neo-classical' economics also?). This does not imply that the new economic dynamics will not leave plenty of scope for, and lay stress on, the advantages of competition and free markets.

We now pass over to the last four charts, showing the upward slope of the warranted growth curve as less than that of the natural growth curve. There are not enough savings in the case of countries, to which this group of charts is applicable, to finance 'natural' growth. One thinks at once of the less developed countries. One should, however, be careful about this. Slow growth in some of these may be due, not so much to a low saving ratio, as to the difficulty of building up an increase of technological know-how and of a personnel well qualified to implement it. It may be interesting to ask which are the countries to which the analysis of the first three diagrams applies and which fall under the last four categories. It is surely the case that the U.S.A. must be regarded as belonging to the excess saving group (charts 1–3).

It is a nice question whether Britain is an over-saving or under-saving country. Keynes certainly thought that it was an over-saver, and it was this that led him to formulate his unemployment theories, and to recommend public works as a recipe in the early 1920s. For most of the inter-war period the British position could probably be represented by chart 3. If this is correct, the Keynesian recommendation of reflation for Britain was good on all three counts.

The position of Britain in this regard since the Second World War is not so clear. She received a frightful knock in the war. On the domestic side the knock was probably not as bad as those sustained by Germany and Holland. But the knock on her external balance of payments was easily the worst in the world; the restoration of an external balance requires super-normal investment. This may account for the poor performance of Britain in the international league tables showing post-war growth of production per caput.

In the most recent period British phenomena seem to have become more like those in the U.S.A., near stagnation in the G.N.P. combined with very strong wage-price spiralling. But it may be that this resemblance is superficial and that Britain is still an under-saver. In the last three years the British Treasury has been actuating a Budget surplus, which is certainly an all-time high for Britain and for any important country in the world. I cannot guarantee that some less important country, may not inadvertently have had an even greater surplus for a short period!

The British Budget surplus reached its peak in 1969–70, at £2,444 million, which was about 6·2 per cent of national income. But for this abnormal governmental saving, the British economy might have appeared as one in which a substantial demand-pull was still operating.

The British authorities have, oddly enough, tended to play down this heroic effort by its taxpayers. They have laid more stress on the Government's 'borrowing requirement'. In 1970–1 the surplus dropped a little to £1,757 m., still an all-time and all-country high, except for the U.K. in 1969/70; the estimate for 1971–2 is for £2,316 m.

The British, by democratic process, decided after the Second World War to nationalise a number of important, and importantly capital-requiring, industries. It also lends large sums to the local authorities. The 'borrowing requirement' is calculated after account has been taken of all these, and some other similar, out-payments. Despite them all the government was able to redeem National Debt to the small extent of £43 million in 1970/1. In 1971/2 it is estimated that there will be a 'borrowing requirement' of £683 million – not a large sum.

Most countries, outside the regimes of socialism, have not nationalised so many industries as has Britain. Capital outlays on behalf of nationalised industries, or on behalf of the local authorities, should not be reckoned as part of 'government expenditure'. Rather they constitute the provision of capital disposal by the Government, as required to finance investments authorised directly or indirectly by it. Before the war persons and companies subscribed out of their savings the sums needed for capital formation in the industries subsequently nationalised. Money subscribed for this purpose by people, whether as investors, as in the old days, or as taxpayers, should be reckoned in the estimate of national savings. Nationalisation makes no difference. Consequently it is the 'Budget surplus' and not 'the borrowing requirement' that should be used in reckoning the government's (taxpayers') contribution to total national saving.

One wonders why British Government spokesmen lay more stress on the 'borrowing requirement' than on the magnificent Budget surplus. The motive is probably related to their constituents. If the true Budget surplus were more widely publicised, there might be a revolt on the part of the taxpayers. 'Why on earth should we pay taxes to finance the capital requirements of various bodies, which, before the war, were financed, in return for interest, by those investors who could afford to do so?' This objection would be absolutely correct. I am confident that the great majority of citizens have no idea of what is happening. It suits the cautious Treasury that they should not be enlightened.

But this policy harms Britain's international reputation. Around the world she is commonly regarded as rather a spendthrift country. In fact in 1969 her saving ratio was as high as 22·6 per cent. These matters are of course correctly set out in the Blue Book on National Income. But not everyone studies this.

However, it remains an open question whether, in the absence of this huge fiscal deflator, Britain could be reckoned as an oversaving country.

In this work on theory I will go no further in attempting to assess the conditions in the various countries. It is usually, and, presumably, correctly, assumed that there is insufficient saving in most of the less developed countries to enable them to achieve their growth potentials, but in their case, as already noted, one must bear in mind that lack of qualified personnel may be the effective bottleneck. There is doubtless undersaving in some advanced countries also.

Diagrams from four to seven, inclusive, represent the undersaving cases, namely where the warranted growth rate is below the natural one. All four are conflict cases. In all those cases the effects of sustained expansionist policies are represented as bad for the long-run growth equilibrium. If they are to achieve their growth potential, these countries need to save more. But sustained reflation is inimical to saving. This is obviously so on the fiscal side – reducing Budget surpluses or increasing deficits. The effects of low interest on personal saving may be doubtful. Sustained low interest will presumably in the long run reduce the normal profit rate. To the extent that a larger proportion of profit is saved than that saved out of other income, as stressed by some economists, such as Professor (Joan) Robinson, a reduction in the regular rate of profit will be bad for saving.

There may once more be mental resistance. Expansionist policies are designed to, and do, increase investment; but investment is equal to saving; therefore they increase saving. That cannot be denied. The point is that, in an undersaving country, an expansionist policy *reduces* the amount of investment that one can have without incurring demand-pull inflation, and, possibly, a consequent increase of wage-price spiralling.

Where there are conflicts, there is no absolutely right policy. It becomes a matter of judgement. This has nothing whatever to do with so-called 'value judgements', a stupid sloppy expression, which has lately been obtruding itself into serious works on economics. Actually, 'value judgement' is an expression that can have no meaning, if one has regard to the proper sense of the two words used in it.[1] The 'judgements' in the case before us relate not to 'value', but to a factual matter, namely to the question which of the alternatives will increase human happiness most – the objective of applied economics. 'Judgement' is

[1] Cf. *Foundations of Inductive Logic* by R. F. Harrod, p. 272.

required because available observations – these are empirical questions – do not give us precise enough information to provide values for the parameters of the equations as required by mathematical economists.

The diagrams do not include the happy case in which all three growth rates have the same slope. Monetary and fiscal policies would still be needed to prevent runaway movements.

In the fourth case the actual growth curve, starting from a full employment position, has a lower gradient than the natural curve; obviously at the full employment position the actual growth curve cannot be above the natural curve. This is subject to the proviso that must always be borne in mind, that the definition of the natural growth curve implies that a certain proportion (probably a growing proportion) of the productive resources of the country should be devoted to providing amenities (preservation of the countryside, etc.) that are left out or under-weighted in the reckoning of the G.D.P. Thus it may happen that actual growth, as measured in G.D.P. terms, exceeds 'natural' growth thus defined. Too many productive resources may be mobilised into producing marketable goods and services, and thus not enough be left over for providing amenities. In fact, this is a phenomenon that occurs quite frequently in advanced countries. Deflation should then be applied to reducing the quantum of demand for marketable goods and services, releasing resources for the provision of amenities. The net effect will be neutral, since the deflationary policies required to reduce demand for marketable goods and services will be offset by greater expenditure on amenities. It is assumed of course that such expenditure is made to take place.

The fact that in graph 4 the actual growth curve has a lower gradient than the natural growth curve entails that in due course unemployment will develop. From this point of view some expansionist policy is needed to maintain full employment. But the actual curve is rising above the warranted curve, so that, unless deflationary measures are adopted, demand-pull inflation will come into being. And so we have a conflict. Either tolerate growing unemployment or adopt measures that will cause demand-pull inflation, which may (or may not) activate wage-price spiralling. The idea that one can have a perfect policy, a sort of 'fine-tuning', that prevents a growth of unemployment on the one hand while not setting up demand-pull price inflation on the other has no basis in economic theory.

There are two things that we need to know in order to resolve the conflict, as so far presented. (There is the further problem arising from column 3.)

1. We need to know the amount of human suffering entailed by an increase of unemployment of, say, 1 per cent above a minimum frictional level, and the amount of suffering caused to fixed income people by an increase in the rate of inflation by, say, 1 per cent above what it would otherwise be. That is a problem within the domain of sociology, about which economists, as such, cannot be expected to be expert. It requires investigation by fieldwork.

2. We need to know in this conflict case what is the actual write-off between the two evils. May the measures, for instance, that are required to prevent an increase of unemployment by 1 per cent entail an increase of price inflation of 3 per cent, due to demand-pull, but possibly also enhanced by the effect of demand pull in increasing the rate of wage-price spiralling? This lies within the sphere of empirical economics. There is obviously no *a priori* answer.

Then we have to have regard to column 3. If expansionist measures have to be maintained for a substantial time, they may reduce the normal warranted growth rate. In the graph it is already, at the opening point, running below the natural growth rate. If it is further reduced, then in future the amount of unemployment or of price inflation that has to be endured from time to time will be further increased. This deserves serious consideration.

The right answer to the immediate problem, subject to more profound empirical investigation, appears to be to endeavour to make the remedial measures quick and snappy. A short bout of inflation, if this is needed to prevent unemployment, should not have an adverse effect on saving propensities. But this is not a long-run solution, since, if the warranted growth rate continues below the natural rate, there will be recurrent problems.

A partial answer to the long-term problem is for the authorities to supplement the private supply of saving by doing saving themselves. This is obviously required in many less developed countries where the saving propensity is weak. By increasing aggregate saving the authorities can render it possible for the warranted growth curve to lie along the natural growth curve and for the country in question to achieve its growth potential.

But what of the short period problem? The chart shows a propensity for unemployment to increase. Extra saving on a substantial scale by the authorities can be done only by taking purchasing power out of the pockets of the citizens, and that will intensify the trend to unemployment. We are at the very heart of the contradiction.

The answer to it is that there is *no* cure by the conventional remedies of monetary and fiscal policies. The authorities must themselves initiate *investments*. Then the withdrawal of purchasing power from the pockets of the citizens, which by itself would tend to create unemployment, will be offset by the earnings of those given employment on the new investment projects. It is no good thinking blithely that by monetary and fiscal policies one can secure full employment and avoid demand-pull inflation. (Wage push inflation is quite a different matter and *clearly* not capable of being controlled by monetary and fiscal policies.) Some economists are still living in a sort of dream world. As against the old-fashioned doctrine of free market capitalism, most of them have conceded that deliberate management by monetary and fiscal policies is desirable. But it is not enough! The doctrine may perhaps be salvaged in relation to countries in which the saving ratio is high, subject to the difficulties that I have discussed in regard to case 2. Where the saving ratio is on the low side (countries 4–7 in the table) the traditional doctrine has to be scrapped. And who can say how many countries in the world spectrum are on the low saving side?

In case 5 expansionist policy is needed both to check an increase of unemployment and to prevent demand deflation. But there remains the countervailing consideration of the long run. Again a sudden burst of expansionism, not prolonged enough to have an effect on the warranted growth rate, would be good; but also once again consideration should be paid to the long-run situation, and again an increase of official saving, accompanied by an increase of official *investment*, would be desirable.

The sixth case is an intensified version of the fourth case. Initial unemployment is postulated. Even so, expansionist monetary and fiscal policies will immediately cause demand-pull price inflation, as in the second case. Presumably here also one ought to have a short-run expansionist policy, with the foot firmly placed on the accelerator to cure unemployment. Some price inflation will then have to be accepted. But here again, to prevent warranted growth slipping still further below natural growth, one needs a substantial increase in fiscal saving accompanied by enough additional official investment to offset that. Case 7 is similar to case 6, except that an expansionist policy will not cause short-run demand price inflation.

In all four cases, in which private saving is insufficient to give a warranted rate of growth equal to what the economy is capable of, it should be supplemented by official saving *and* official investment of like amount. A mere Budget surplus will not cause countries in these stances to move in the right way. A parallel increase of investment is also required. In the foregoing I have referred to this extra investment as investment by the official authorities. That is probably appropriate for many countries, especially the less developed. It may be that in more advanced countries, the same effect could be achieved by subsidies to private investment. This method would not yield so sure a result. Subsidies to investment have been becoming rather popular recently, especially in the high saving countries. But in these countries they are not appropriate.

There may still be mental resistance. In low-saving countries it may be granted that private savings should be supplemented by official savings. But, that done, why not let private enterprise get on with the job of putting the extra investment that can be financed by the extra saving into operation? The trouble is that private enterprise may lack a motive for doing so. In order to hoist total savings to an appropriate level, the authorities reduce the buying power of citizens. Private enterprise producers are confronted with a shrunken demand for their products. That is not a good background against which they are likely to decide to step up their investment. Consider a country like India where the saving ratio has been notably low. The Government quite rightly decides to supplement private saving. In the very process of doing so, it must reduce the increase in demand for consumer goods. This will reduce the incentive to private enterprise to sustain its previous pace of investment, let alone increase it. Or, to go on to more controversial ground, consider Russia. The socialist view was that there had not been sufficient expansion under the Tsarist regime. It may well be that the socialists took too poor a view of what the Tsarist rule had actually achieved for Russia in the early twentieth century; that is a side-issue. Quite apart from the general socialist doctrine that the Government must decide upon and initiate everything, there was the more particular view that Russia needed a much higher rate of investment. In the early days the regime was criticised for laying too much stress on the basic capital-producing industries at the cost of considerable hardship to poor consumers. But when the Second World War came, their allies were thankful that they had done so; it helped them to produce the munitions of war. In the last decade they have shifted their emphasis on to consumer goods.

We have here another illustration of the principle that is so vitally important in human affairs. If each one separately does something, that will bring him no advantage; but if a large number simultaneously do it, they will all benefit. In an underdeveloped society there may be no method of getting a large number, independently and simultaneously, to do what is needful; if the thing is to be done on a relevant scale, the Government may have to do it.

It is to be feared that no tidy set of solutions has been provided for the various conflict cases set out in the table of charts. The conflicts are real, and cannot just be thought away.

The use of monetary and fiscal policies in various connections has been considered. It has throughout been assumed that these policies can often not have any substantial effect on cost-push inflation which may degenerate into wage price spiralling. To deal with this, a totally different kind of weapon is needed, namely direct interference, whether on a voluntary or mandatory basis, with the fixing of prices and wages, commonly called an 'incomes policy'. Traditional monetary and fiscal policies have quite enough complex problems with which to deal, without having that one also put on their plate. It is possible that at times demand-pull inflation may cause wage-price spiralling to be higher than it would otherwise be. In that case an elimination of the demand-pull inflation might reduce the pace of wage-price spiralling. In this connection it should be recalled that there can be demand-pull inflation, even when unemployment is substantially above the frictional level. We have seen that in some of the conflict cases, it may be desirable to tolerate some demand-pull inflation, e.g. in order to reduce unemployment. This choice will be simplified if there is assurance that the wage-price spiralling is being looked after by another method, viz. an 'incomes policy'. That will simplify the choice between a moderate demand-pull inflation and leaving in being a substantial degree of unnecessary employment.

To allow the possibility that an elimination of demand-pull inflation may – the matter is not certain – in some cases reduce the rate of wage-price spiralling, does not imply that this elimination will also eliminate the wage-price spiralling. The latter frequently occurs when there is no demand-pull inflation in progress, and accordingly it must not be postulated that the elimination of demand-pull inflation will be a cure for price-inflation. The idea that the amount of inflation (*simpliciter*) is a direct function of the level of employment (the 'Phillips curve') is not acceptable. The rate of wage-price spiralling is primarily a sociological matter, not dependent on market forces. This is not to deny that, if demand deflation is pushed to the extent of producing a really formidable level of unemployment, say 20 per cent, it may bring wage-price spiralling to a halt. This is because a crisis atmosphere will have been created; the curative effect of this is a sociological phenomenon, and not one consequent upon the operation of market forces. Unless the need for an 'incomes policy' is agreed upon and one is activated, we cannot hope for an acceptable solution of the price-inflation problem. Meanwhile it should obviously not be within the scheme of regular policy in sophisticated societies that unemployment should be increased from time to time to a level that creates a crisis atmosphere. So in any rational planning we must assume that the tendency of wage-price spiralling to develop is being looked after by other methods and cannot be expected to be controlled by the recognised monetary and fiscal policies.

I would stress two points in the foregoing analysis of the different cases. The problems of a country that tends to generate more saving than it can usefully employ on net investment are obviously less acute than those of a country that is not saving enough. In regard to the former, a conflict appears only in one of the three possible cases illustrated in the charts (case 2). In this case it is essential that taxes should be reduced, either moderately or heavily, depending on the amount of over-saving, at the *top* of the boom, when employment is at its maximum or even over-stretched. There is a paradox in this. But the correct theory of applied economies is full of paradoxes. That is probably why economic policy has recently been so lame. Unsophisticated thinking tends to suppose that the right time to reduce taxes is when the economy is in a phase of stagnation or recession. This is wrong. The right time to reduce taxes is when unemployment is at its minimum and there is the probability, near certainty, that it will in due course begin to increase. For this purpose the responsible authorities should be all lined up and ready to reduce taxes as soon as, or, preferably, before, unemployment shows any signs of increasing. For right judgement about this relevant point of time information is needed. It may on occasion happen during the phase preceding full employment that saving and investment are both supernormal and that some decline is inevitable. But the actual decline may be excessive. Such excessive declines have been acquiesced in, as something likely to happen. But if, at the appropriate point, taxation had been promptly reduced at the top of the boom, so as to keep the demand for end-products growing at a rate appropriate to the country's high saving ratio, the amount of investment needed by consequence, and planned and undertaken, would not have declined so much.

The second point concerns undersaving countries. In the relevant cases, in my judgement, it is needful for the authorities themselves to undertake additional investment of significant amount. It is appropriate for the authorities to supplement the low private savings by official savings, so as to ensure that in such countries there is enough total saving to finance, without demand inflation, the investment needed to maintain growth of output commensurate with the potential of the economies in question. But this very supplementation of saving (increase of taxes above the current level or above what is expected to be required for governmental expenditures on current account), will reduce the purchasing power in the pocket of the purchasers of goods. Accordingly wise heads will be led to expect a decline, or abatement in the rate of increase, of the demands for what they produce. Accordingly they will not have a motive for stepping up their rate of investment previously planned; rather the other way round. In these circumstances, if there is to be increased investment, as needed to balance the increase of saving caused by budget surpluses, the official authorities must themselves actuate that increase. Otherwise it will not happen. The increased savings, intended to be obtained by the increase of taxation relatively to government expenditure, will just be water spilt on the ground, in the famous words of D. H. Robertson; the increased governmental saving will be offset by diminished company saving due to the decline in company profit. Failing additional government investment, company profit will decline by whatever is needed to keep the decrease of company saving equal to the increase of governmental saving, so that there will be no net increase of saving.

At this point a word should be said about what has been called 'Indicative Planning'. This idea had a vogue for some time, but recently less has been heard about it. In my judgement this has gone along with a decline in the quality of economic thinking in the more recent period. The vogue for indicative planning has been superseded by quite unacceptable doctrines, put out by the so-called monetarist school of economists. I hasten to repeat that I am myself a great believer in the potent influence on growth that can be exercised by an appropriate regulation of the money supply. I hope that these pages have demonstrated that. But the idea that increasing the money supply at a suitable rate can solve all the problems of growth is perfect nonsense. The problems with which the theory of growth, in accordance with potential, are involved are much more complex than that.

The country that raised itself most by the concept of Indicative Planning was France. The French growth rate, based on the policy of Indicative Planning, was probably, at the time when it obtained, foremost in the world. Germany may have come near to rivalling it; but, as we know from past experience, countries defeated in war usually do better in the following period than those victorious. Maxim (apparently!): 'If possible, be defeated in a war.' (Compare Germany and Japan since 1945.)

The idea of 'indicative planning' is to establish what growth is achievable over a coming, say, five-year period. The central authorities do some sums and then write around to representatives of the various industries. Naturally the calculations involve higher growth rates in some sectors than in others. The authorities seek to know from each industry whether the growth rate implied for it is feasible. From some industries they may get the reply: 'We can do better than that'; from others they may get a negative reply: 'We do not think that we can increase so much.'

On the basis of such replies, the 'indicative plan' may be modified, and renewed questions be sent out. Ideally there should be a good deal of to and fro, until the maximum feasible growth plan was roughly agreed by the different sectors. Actually the process will not, presumably, be carried on to this extreme. But an official plan will be decided upon that seems more or less feasible.

The objective is that this final plan shall seem, within limits, more or less feasible to the various sectors, and that they will *act* upon it.

The 'plan' should indicate roughly what amount of increase of demand each sector may expect. This may be larger than each would expect in the absence of the plan. So each sector, having confidence that there will be a greater expansion across-the-board of demand than there would be in the absence of the plan, makes more investment than it otherwise would. The government, on its side, undertakes to increase its own demand, which may be of important significance, by as much as is indicated by the framework of the plan. This gives the private sector an important prop in relation to what it is expected to do.

Thus in cases in which private enterprise does not, on the overall average, believe that market demand will, if left to itself, rise sufficiently to justify the overall average desirable rate of increase, 'indicative planning' may provide a compromise between letting the growth rate fall below its optimum and keeping it up to that optimum solely by government investment (socialism) taking over the function of producing additional capital goods as needed to secure 'natural' growth.

Monetary and fiscal policies can, together, ensure a growth of aggregate demand in accordance with supply potential of the economy; but they cannot always do so without entailing demand-pull inflation. 'Indicative planning' may possibly be able to do this, and in this respect it is a weapon of superior sophistication.

8 Foreign Trade

By early traditional economics external payments were supposed to come into balance automatically. If a metallic standard was in operation and notes were convertible, gold or silver would flow in or out and make up the difference between the plusses and minuses of international payments, when these were not in balance. These flows operated on the domestic price level by changing the size of the internal money supply. An outward flow would depress domestic prices, thereby stimulating exports and discouraging imports, and conversely. This process would reduce and finally eliminate the external gap, at which point the flow of metal would cease.

If notes were not convertible and there was an external imbalance, the foreign exchange rate would move away from the official parity. It was the downward case that was usually considered. This would have the same effect on the external balance as a downward movement of domestic prices; it would render home produced goods cheaper for the foreigner and home made goods relatively cheaper for the domestic buyer. The exchange rate would move to whatever level was needed, to secure balance.

In the course of time it came to be held that some intervention by the authorities might be needed, in the case where notes were convertible, if convertibility was to be preserved. With the development of the banking system and the growth of bank deposits the precious metals came to constitute a progressively smaller fraction of the total money supply in each country. Thus the reduction of that total supply due to an outflow of metal might not be proportionally large enough to bring prices down sufficiently to cure the imbalance. The gold (or silver) reserve might be eliminated or reduced to an inconveniently low level, while yet the imbalance continued. Then convertibility might have to be suspended. It was usually considered that everything must be done to avoid this, except, perhaps, in the case of a major war.

Accordingly, the authorities came to feel that it was their duty to take action to speed up the adjustment process by reducing the other elements in the total domestic money supply, namely bank money in its various forms. This seemed to round off the doctrine about how a smoothly working monetary system could be maintained.

But two very serious questions have to be raised, in relation to the working of this seemingly elegant system.

One may be called the Keynesian criticism. It is a matter to which he devoted particular attention in the early twenties; it also had its influence all through his later thinking. On the occasion of an external deficit, the authorities speed up the adjustment process by reducing the supply of bank money. The central bank does this by means of raising the bank rate and reducing various forms of lending. This is supposed to bring down prices to a level consistent with external equilibrium. But it also does something else, and, in Keynes's view, that something else is considerably more important. In the process of reducing the money supply it makes borrowing by industry more difficult; this will tend to reduce the orders that industry can place and the new activities that it can set in motion, and this in turn will tend to reduce employment. A tight money policy may have considerably more effect, he held, in reducing employment, than it has in bringing prices down. Furthermore, its effect in improving the external balance, which is not denied, may operate more strongly via its reduction of *real* income and thereby the power of citizens to purchase foreign goods than via any fall of domestic prices that may occur. So is this system after all so elegant and admirable as proponents of the gold standard claimed it to be? May not a system that secures adjustment by exchange rate changes be preferable?

Incidentally, we have already seen the very complex problems confronting monetary management in relation to the various positions of the three growth rates. In that treatment no reference was made to the external balance. We shall need to examine in due course whether the problem of the external balance gives rise to further conflicts.

The second question relating to the 'elegant' classical theory of the external balance is concerned with price elasticities of demand. The traditional theory is that a fall of home prices relative to foreign prices will improve the external balance. As is now well known, this implies that the sum of the price elasticity of foreign demand for home goods and of the price elasticity of the home demand for foreign goods is greater than one. It can be slightly less, if the initial position is one of deficit for the home country. There is no *a priori* reason why the sum of those elasticities should be as high as this. Wise economists have been inclined to take the view that, while their sum might well be too low in the short period, it is likely to be substantially in excess of one in the longer period. But the trouble is that various frustrating events may have occurred before the long period is reached.

The British in the nineteenth century reposed calmly on the traditional doctrine, and seem to have managed their balance of payments problems sufficiently well. This enabled them to adhere rigidly to the policy of Free Trade. It is to be noted, however, that the British relied heavily on monetary action to influence international capital movements; in regard to these they had a very important position in the world scene. Other countries seem to have felt the need to alter protectionist impediments from time to time in relation to their balance of payments positions. Some might argue that this was because their economics were backward and they had not yet understood the overriding benefits of Free Trade; or, again, it could be argued that they had not yet begun to understand how a proper regulation of the money supply could maintain an equal balance of payments. There is the other alternative. It may be that the price elasticities of demand were not sufficiently great, and that many countries had a hunch that this was so; it may be that the British got away with Free Trade, not because the price elasticities were sufficiently great, but because of their more influential position in the international capital market. International capital movements will be analysed in the next chapter.

The above has given some general remarks within the sphere of macro-statics. It is next needful to proceed to dynamic theory in relation to the foreign trade balance. For this purpose it may be useful to consider the matter in terms of a few very broad categories.

We may begin with imports of food. Imports have to be considered both in relation to income growth and the trend of relative prices. Income growth divides into that due to population increase and that due to overall productivity increase. In the case of food one would suppose, in a country normally substantially dependent on food imports, the component of food inport increase due to population increase to have elasticity greater than one. The marginal incremental requirements for food will have a higher proportion devoted to imports than in the case of demand for food as a whole. To put it crudely, the fraction of its population that a country can feed from its own production declines.

On the other hand there may be a productivity growth in the domestic production of food greater than the population growth. In such a case, the growth of food imports associated with the population growth may decline and indeed may even fall below the population growth rate.

The effect of the element of overall productivity growth in the total growth of national income on the demand for food will probably be markedly different as between poorer and richer countries. In the case of very poor countries the income per caput elasticity of the demand for food may even exceed unity. When a little extra income comes in to very poor underfed families, living in their shacks, with a minimum of clothing and no goods beyond bare necessities, they may think it a good idea to give priority to having some more food. The whole of incremental income may be devoted to food, or, anyhow, a proportion of it that is larger than the proportion of their total income devoted to food, giving an income elasticity of the demand for food greater than unity. Of course the rise in their own incomes may be simply due to their increased production of food; this is subsistence economy; they produce more food and consume the extra that they have produced. But even in the poorest countries there will be some not engaged wholly in the production of food, and productivity may rise in spheres other than food production. That may or may not be balanced by the increased productivity of food producers who produce surpluses not consumed by themselves. We shall deal with exports presently. There have been notable cases where the higher domestic consumption of food has had its main impact on exports, rather than on imports.

In the case of richer countries, the income elasticity of the demand for food tends to be below unity. The people have enough to eat. Doubtless they seek for higher-quality food and more tasty varieties. But they are likely to raise their non-food spending more than in proportion to their food spending.

The productivity element in the income elasticity of demand for food imports depends on (*a*) the ratio of productivity growth in agriculture to productivity growth generally and (*b*) the ratio of food consumption currently supplied by home production. The lower these ratios, the higher the income (as dependent on productivity) elasticity of demand for food imports will be.

The question of price elasticity must be considered. The standard types of food are marketed in conditions of perfect competition and have world prices. This is not to say that they have the same prices in the various countries. On the contrary, food is notoriously subject to national regulations and heavy trade restrictions. It is largely exempt from normal GATT rules in regard to those. One has to add also the normal obstacles to the tendency of prices to equality in different countries – transport costs, etc.

The traditional view of balance of payments equilibrium was that, in the case of a deficit, the outflow of gold, that being reinforced by a suitable contraction of bank money, would depress domestic prices relatively to foreign prices. In the case of goods with world prices, the contraction of the local money supply will not have any effect on their domestic prices. There will be no consequential price differential, as between domestic and foreign prices, tending to redress the external balance; nor will fiscal policy tend to produce such a differential. Again, if an adjustment in the external balance is sought through an alteration in the exchange rate, import prices will rise and domestic prices will do so in the same proportion, unless there is a parallel change in the amount of domestic subsidies or protection. It is arguable, however, that the greater rise in food prices compared with other prices in the home market might give some encouragement to the domestic production of food.

Thus neither a change in domestic monetary and fiscal policies nor a change in the foreign exchange rate will have any effect on food imports via price elasticity of demand. The former will of course have some effect via income elasticity.

The main instrument for getting an important change in food imports is direct regulation.

In the U.K. the growth rate of food imports has been very moderate recently. The volume index rose from 102 in 1965 to 104 in 1970 (base: 1961 = 100). To check on this statistical computation, it is possible to take the actual import figures corrected by the unit value index. By this method one gets an increase of real food imports over the whole period between 1965 and 1970 of 3 per cent. The figures are sufficiently similar, and one may have confidence that the growth rate of food imports in this period was very low indeed. In the same period the volume of all imports rose from 120 to 157 (base: 1961). The increase of the Gross Domestic Product at constant prices (1963) rose by 10·9 per cent. It is evident enough that food imports were rising at a much lower growth rate than national income.

The main reasons for this are (i) the notable increase in domestic agricultural productivity and (ii) the fall in the ratio of the value of food consumption to national income. The index of food consumption in this five-year period rose by 6·9 per cent (1963 prices), which was substantially below the increase of real national income in the same period.

The principles governing the growth of imports of raw materials are not very different. We have similar reasons for (1) on the one hand expecting a slower growth rate in the demand for raw materials than in total income. As people grow richer, a smaller fraction of income is devoted to buying a greater mass of raw material, and a larger fraction to working it up into final products of higher quality and agreeable variety, and also to services. On the other side, (2) diminishing returns to scale will be present, as in the case of food, but imposing a stronger constraint on increased domestic production. If dependence on imports is substantial, the income elasticity of demand for them will tend to rise for the same reason as in the case of food.

Between 1965 and 1970 imports of basic materials in the U.K. rose from 107 to 110 only (base: 1961). In this category there are apt to be greater fluctuations up and down. In the three-year period from 1965 to 1967 inclusive the index stood at 103·5 while in the period 1968–70 it stood at 109·7. It is clear that this category as recorded had a notably low growth rate.

There may be an element of deception here however. Some goods may have passed over from the category of basic materials to that of manufactures for further processing. There has been a tendency for less developed countries to apply the first stages of processing to their basic material products before exporting them, which transfers them from the category of basic materials into that of manufactures for further processing. This is a natural tendency in their early stages of development and has also in cases been a matter of governmental policy.

The price elasticity of the demand for the category as a whole is likely to be low. The materials are needed for the production of goods, of which, however, they are usually only a minor part of the cost. Doubtless a substantial rise in the price of a particular material may in certain cases lead to an earnest search for a substitute or other methods of economising its use in the productive process: and conversely. The range for such substitutions is probably limited. But an overall average rise (or fall) in the prices of imported materials, as caused, for instance, by a devaluation, is hardly likely to have a significant effect in promoting a switch into (or out of) material goods into services, the provision of which has a lower material content. If there is in fact a higher rate of increase in the use of rising income to buy services than in its use to buy material goods, that will depend on more fundamental causes – the evolving desires and tastes of consumers.

Passing reference may be made to a foolish tax introduced in Britain, called the Selective Employment Tax, a few years ago. The incidence of the tax raised the cost of employing labour on services, while not that of doing so in industrial production. In so far as it had any effect at all, it would *raise* Britain's import bill at a time when she had rather important balance of payments difficulties. It was argued that the tax would release labour from the services to produce more exports. That could have been done in other ways; and it was not clear at that time that actual exports were held down to a significant extent by delayed delivery; rather it was owing to insufficiently competitive prices or failure to keep abreast with changing world requirements. It was also argued by some that the switch of labour would raise the national growth rate, on the ground that, when industrial production grows by a certain amount, it is possible to increase productivity in that sphere by more than can be done in the services when they grow by an equal amount. Thus the switch would make total national income grow more than it otherwise would.

It must be strongly stressed that this is not in conformity with the idea of a natural growth rate as properly defined. An appeal must at this point be made to classical economics; its conclusions remain valid; they must not be thrown out of the window. Dynamics has its own contributions to make, but classical economics remains important. It holds that the optimum is secured when individuals can choose freely among goods, priced in proportion to their real costs of production. If prices are distorted away from this pattern, then the individual will get less satisfaction in the spending of his income than he otherwise would. The target of growth policy is to maximise the growth of the *satisfaction* of people. Natural growth has been defined in this volume as the maximum growth of production of goods and services that can be achieved by the growth of the working population – subject to increasing leisure, if desired – and technological progress. It was implied that this maximum refers to the production of goods and services that people most want, not to any job lot of goods. The S.E.T. idea that the G.N.P. can be increased by subsidising the production of material goods, as against services, can be reduced to absurdity. Find out the article in the production of which technological progress is currently greatest. Tell the consumers that they can have this good and none other at all. Then you will have maximised the national growth rate!

To summarise, the income elasticity of demand for imported basic materials is normally below unity; it may rise somewhat through time if the domestic economy can produce some of them in limited quantities, but with sharply diminishing returns for greater quantities. The price elasticity is likely to be low. Accordingly exchange rate variations are likely to have only a negligible effect on this class of imports. As regards deflationary monetary and fiscal policies, if these are introduced when aggregate demand is in excess of the supply potential of the economy, they are not likely to have any effect on this class of imports. But if they are kept in being after aggregate demand has fallen below the supply potential, or if they are introduced then for whatever reason, they will have some appreciable effect on this class of imports. The amount of these imports is mainly a function of the activity of the economy. It must be borne in mind that they are subject to rather important time-lags.

We may pass over to the class of imports that is at the other end of the spectrum – finished manufactures. They may be expected to be income-elastic. As people get richer, they spend a larger proportion of their income on high-wrought articles and become more choosey. Inevitably, if they cast their eyes around the world, they will find a wider range of choice than if they look at domestic products only. Thus, as their incomes grow, they will spend a growing proportion of the increments on foreign products. This entails an-income elasticity of demand for imports of finished manufactures that is greater than unity.

It seems clear that in the U.K. there has in recent years been a specific change of taste, namely a growing preference for foreign goods *as such*. This is different from the wider considera-tion explained in the last paragraph. There the high income-elasticity was due to greater choosiness among sophisticated articles and shopping around the world to find the best. A specific preference for foreign goods, because they are foreign, is slightly different. The same phenomenon seems to have occurred in the U.S.A. This is a once-over change, albeit one that could continue to proceed for a number of years or even decades. While the proportion of income devoted to buying objects that imply shopping round the world will continue to increase until everyone in the nation is as rich as Croesus, the preference for foreign goods as such would seem to be a transitory phase of fashion. It does not make sense to suppose that a preference for foreign goods, simply because they are foreign, would continue indefinitely to be a positive function of a rising income.

In this category price-elasticity is likely to be high. If foreign goods almost identical with the domestic product become more expensive relatively to the domestic product, the purchases of them will fall off; and conversely.

Finished manufactures include capital goods – machinery, transport equipment, etc. In the British case imported finished capital goods have recently had more than twice the value of imported finished consumer goods. In the case of finished capital goods one would expect high price-elasticity.

In the recent British experience the other considerations seem to have outweighed any price-elasticity that there may have been. Between 1965 and 1970 the monthly average value of imports of finished manufactures rose from £74 million to £171 million (131·1 per cent). The rise has been, although not regular, continuing and progressive, and there is nothing to suggest that 1970 was a freak year. National income (money value), rose by 36·6 per cent only. In this period the price index of imported manufactures rose from 109 to 142, an increase of 30 per cent. If we may apply this price index to finished manufactures,[1] we get an increase in the volume of these imports of 77 per cent. The rise of real national income in this period was 11 per cent only.

Meanwhile the price index of domestic manufactures rose from 106 to 128, an increase of 20·8 per cent. Thus, so far as prices were conserned, there should have been a switch to the domestic products. But the other considerations outweighed this factor. This kind of British experience, which extends back beyond 1965 – but, if one goes too far back, the scene is muddled by remaining post-war import restrictions and the consequences of their removal – may have been exceptional; but it was probably not entirely so. Since one would expect this category of imports to be the most price-elastic, the British example should strike a note of caution about regarding exchange rate flexibility as a panacea for the adjustment of external imbalances in all cases. Furthermore, it suggests that, had the wage-price spiralling, a pernicious evil in itself, been less, the external balance, as influenced by imports, would have been no better.

Semi-finisheds ('manufactures for further processing') are betwixt and between basic materials and finished manufactures. At the end of the spectrum where they most resemble basics, one would expect a strong correlation between their growth,

---

[1] The official statistics do not give separate price or volume index numbers for manufactures for further processing and finished manufactures. If any inaccuracy was involved in using the price index of imported manufactures to deflate the value of imports of finished manufactures, using this index also to deflate the value of imports of manufactures for further processing necessarily involves an equal and opposite mistake; thus the *general* picture remains the same.

subject to time-lags, and that of real national income, but with an income-elasticity of demand of less than unity. One would expect their price-elasticity of demand to be rather low, although not quite so low as that for basics. Note has already been taken, in the case of Britain, of the effect of increased elementary processing in the less developed countries of goods previously classified as basic materials, so that some imported objects passed out of that category into that of 'manufactures for further processing'. This partly accounts for the very sluggish increase of the imports of basics into Britain in the period and the very strong increase of manufactures for further processing. This change-over probably affects the external balances of all developed countries. From their points of view the effect is adverse, but from a world point of view it is benign, for two reasons: (i) the marginal utility of income is lower in the less developed countries, so that a transfer of income to them from the developed countries, as a result of their processing raw materials, brings net advantage in terms of human happiness; (ii) the processing of raw materials at a fairly elementary level may be an indispensable step towards the development of more sophisticated manufacturing processes in the less developed countries. The idea that the main trading relation between the less developed countries and those more advanced shall continue indefinitely to be a swapping of food and basics for manufactures is, of course, totally obsolete.

At the other end of the spectrum of manufactures for further processing one may have goods that are near cousins to finished manufactures. In the case of these one might expect a price-elasticity of demand above unity.

In the British case the rate of increase of imports of manufactures for further processing in the period reviewed was very high, although not so high as that of finished manufactures. In the five-year period the value of imported manufactures for further processing rose by 84 per cent. This was considerably less than the rise in the value of finished manufactures (131·1 per cent), but out of all proportion to the general array of British growth rates. If we deflate for the rise in the prices of imported manufactures in this period, we get a volume increase of 39·5 per cent. Again this is far above the general run of real growth rates, but greatly below that for imports of finisheds.

The transfer of some basics into the category of manufactures for further processing can account only for a minor part of this increase. Once again one must suppose that the kind of causes operative in the movement out of British finished manufactures into foreign were operative also in the case of manufactures for further processing at the end of the spectrum nearer to finisheds. This reinforces the need for caution as regards the assumption that exchange rate flexibility will necessarily help to correct an adverse balance by its influence on imports.

When we go over to exports, the primary consideration must be the state of the outside world. Is it in boom or slump? Its status in this respect is the most important factor determining the rate of growth (or decline) of the exports of the home country. Its exports will not normally be evenly dispersed around the world; it will have a greater interest in some countries than in others. Accordingly, it is the state of affairs in the former that is of more significance.

If the growth rate of exports increases, when there is full employment at home, this will cause demand-pull inflation, unless counter-measures are taken. We must consider the various cases in turn.

In a general way it may be said that an increase of export opportunities does not by itself alter either the natural or the warranted growth rates, save via the influence of improved 'terms of trade'. But if the goods for which there is a higher export demand are currently subject to technological progress that is above the average in the economy, this will raise its natural growth rate. The opposite may also occasionally be the case; the extra foreign demand may be for standard items, materials perhaps, in which the technological progress proceeding is subnormal. This will keep productive resources tied down to the relatively stagnant sector and prevent their participating in the more exciting parts of the economy. We may think of British coal exports, 1900–13.

As regards the warranted rate, it will be influenced only if the goods in question are produced by more (or less) capital-intensive methods than the average. If they are produced by more capital-intensive methods, this will reduce the warranted growth rate, and conversely. It will be recalled that there is no necessary connection between sectors where technological progress is above the average and those whose capital intensity is above the average.

In cases 1 and 3 of the charts on page 104, zooming exports will reduce or eliminate the need for reflation; we have what is called an export led boom. In the case of chart 2, the initial conflict will be intensified. The progress towards full employment will be speeded up, but at the same time the demand-pull inflation already under weigh will be increased. The choice is as before. Do we want to get rid of the unemployment as quickly as possible at the cost of a higher rate of demand-pull inflation? There is sometimes confused thinking at this point, it being suggested that an export-led boom is normally less price inflationary than a domestic-led boom. The demand-pull inflation is due to the fact that the actual growth rate is currently running above the warranted rate.

Then we come to the crisis. The higher growth (or level) of exports will not avert it nor the need for tax reduction on a suitable scale. The crisis is caused in the conditions of chart 2 by the fact that, when the ceiling of full employment is reached or approached, the actual rate is inevitably pulled below the warranted rate. In conditions of full, or near-full employment, the actual rate cannot be above the natural rate; but the natural rate is below the warranted rate; therefore the actual rate must fall below the warranted rate and a recession must ensue.

There is, however, the possibility of mitigation. If the extra exports drew on sectors in which technological progress was more rapid than on average in the economy, that would raise the natural rate; and if the exports drew on sectors in which capital intensity was higher than on average in the economy, that would reduce the warranted rate. (It is to be repeated that exports need not have both or either of these characteristics.) If they had them, then there would be a benign coming together of the two rates (natural and warranted) and the amount of tax reduction required to prevent recession would be less. It could indeed happen that the exports made the two rates come right together with equal slopes; that would indeed be a blissful outcome. The economy could then proceed indefinitely without demand inflation or unemployment – until some new disturbance of substantial magnitude occurred to destroy the happy scene.

If, on the whole, rising exports tend to have benign effects, as described, in cases 1–3, then they will have malign effects in cases 4–7. It must be stressed, however, that they are 'malign' only in relation to problems and conflicts. It cannot but be good in the 'absolute' sense, if increased export opportunities raise the natural growth rate, since this means raising the potentiality of increasing happiness. But, when the warranted growth is below the natural growth rate, an increase in the latter pulls them further apart and thus intensifies the problems consequent on their being apart. If a less developed country is confronted with a growth of demand for specific products in which it has a comparative advantage (classical economics), and if increased production of them requires investment in excess of the overall average in its national output, then the requirement for saving is raised and the gap between optimum saving, as needed for the natural growth rate, and desired saving is increased. A greater supplementation to saving by Budget surplus will be needed. This will reduce the domestic demand for consumer products. This will not be fully offset by the increased demand for exports, unless the capital-output ratio is as low as one. Thus the need for *public* investment, to supplement private investment, will be increased. The idea that rising export opportunities will decrease the need for public investment in the less developed countries is illusory.

It may be that in the more sophisticated, but still undersaving, countries, subsidising private investment would be a reasonable, and, if so, desirable, substitute for public investment. That is possible. I have always been doubtful whether the provision of subsidies for investment, at times when the market demand for goods and services is below what the economy can already supply on the overall average, will serve to increase investment. That has always been my personal intuition, and I have not had it contradicted in the many discussions that I have had with industrialists. If they can foresee, or if their best guess is, that the demand for their products within the relevant time-horizon will be sufficient to justify extra investment, they will make it. But if they do not foresee such an increase, subsidies will not induce them to make unnecessary investment. Yet, time and again, in Britain, over a number of years, there has been a simultaneous combination of measures to encourage investment with measures to damp down consumption in an already underemployed economy – the latter designed to rectify an external imbalance or to check price inflation. I have had the sense, in the case of many discussants, that I detected a note of puritanism. 'Consumption is bad; investment is good.' Such an attitude makes no sense; and it is also highly irresponsible. Before taking a view on such a topic, it is needful to try to understand how the economic system works. Such a combination of damping consumption and stimulating investment could in certain circumstances reduce national incomes and thereby the incomes of poor people. Even puritans must surely have a heart for the latter. But actually such people have no zeal for discovery; they are content to utter unsubstantiated, but well sounding, aphorisms.

In the case of undersaving countries (i.e. warranted growth less than natural growth), among which may have to be included some advanced countries, it is desirable that private saving should be supplemented by governmental saving. The latter can be achieved only through reducing, by extra taxation, the purchasing power in the hands of the citizens. This will confront industry with a diminished demand for what it is already able to produce; industry will then have no motive for additional investment. In this case some *governmental* investment is required to keep the system ticking over.

Some governmental authorities in less developed countries may, and should, actuate investment, because they (rightly) believe that their citizens lack the relevant know-how. The governments themselves may be able to hire it, e.g. from the U.S.A.

But the dilemma may arise even in advanced countries. You decrease the buying power of citizens, while expecting industry to step up its rate of investment. We may revert here to the idea of Indicative Planning, already explained. If industry has confidence that the Plan will be carried through, it may make the investments appropriate to the planned expansion of demand for its products over a five-year period, even although the current demand is stagnant. But if Indicative Planning is not acceptable or operable, the Government itself should undertake investment.

In the poorer countries it may be sufficiently obvious that the Government should make investments designed to produce a greater flow of goods and services to its citizens or to provide the capital goods required for that purpose. But in the richer, yet undersaving, countries, we may get a happy consilience between the need for the government to save more, and also to invest more, so as to raise the warranted to a level with the natural growth rate, and the ideas of Professor Kenneth Galbraith. Let the governmental investment take the form of the provision of public amenities.

The point is this. In the undersaving, but relatively rich, countries, it is impossible continuously to maintain full employment by standard monetary and fiscal policies without generating demand-pull inflation. Saving can be supplemented only by governmental surplus, viz. by raising tax receipts. But this will diminish the incentive to industry to invest, owing to the reduction of purchasing power in the hands of buyers. So there is the danger that the additional saving will run into the sand and be lost. Then let the Government use its surplus to make investments on its own account. The compression of demand owing to higher taxes will cause some people to be thrown out of work. But that number will be given work on the Galbraith-type projects.

Of course, in over-saving countries such projects can, and should, be financed by Government borrowing.

Going over to the various categories of goods, we may first consider food exports. The world demand for food grows, both because of increasing population and higher income per caput (higher productivity). The element in the world demand for food that is due to increasing population presumably has an income elasticity equal to one; the element that is due to higher income per person divides, as already explained, into that in which the income elasticity is greater than one and that in which it is less than one. It seems probable that the latter predominates. Around the world there has been a trek out of employment in agriculture. Meanwhile agricultural productivity has been rising, and probably more than overall average productivity. Supply and demand will continue in balance, if the excess rise in agricultural productivity plus the net shortfall of the income elasticity of demand for food are together sufficient to offset the decline in the proportion of the population employed in agriculture.

If world demand tends to rise relatively to supply, this will be reflected in a rise in food prices, and conversely. This trend will cut across regulations in individual countries as regards food prices.

Such a rise in prices on the overall average will increase the value of food exports. By how much it does so depends on the country's own elasticity of supply. Even if the elasticity were zero, there would be some increase in the value of food exports. Indeed, even if the elasticity were below zero – the farmers slacking off when they could earn money more easily – there could still be an improvement. But the margin would not be great, because, owing to transport costs, etc., the main brunt of the 'slacking off' would probably fall on exports.

If the domestic demand for food had some price elasticity, that would help exports.

Food prices are, of course, much influenced by harvest variations. These may affect only a particular food product. But there are reported to be years of across-the-board good or bad harvests. We may be reminded once again of Jevons' sun spots. These variations are not much relevant to the analysis of the mutual interaction of growth trends. But they are highly relevant to the question of the adequacy of world reserves for international settlement. It is monstrous to have a system working by which a country has to alter its development and investment plans, just because it has a bad harvest, or because the rest of the world has supernormal harvests of a commodity of great interest to it, so that its price and the export revenues of the country fall. It is to be added that there are often runs of years of bad harvests. The same argument applies.

Similar considerations are relevant in the case of raw materials. The world income elasticity of demand for them as governed by population increase is likely to be unity and as governed by productivity increase, in respect of all goods and services, below unity. In the case of non-agricultural materials one need not suppose a systematic spontaneous trend of population out of their production. But if the increase of productivity is as great as that in respect of all goods and services on average, there will be an induced movement out of their production. The price elasticities of both demand and supply are likely to be low, so that one may expect world imbalances between supply and demand to cause rather large price oscillations.

These will have strong effects, upwards or downwards, on the value of exports and thereby on the balance of payments, a matter not yet discussed. The effect on the volume of this class of exports and thereby on the quantum of resources devoted to their production is likely to be much smaller. The value effect will lead, via the multiplier, to an increase, or decrease, in domestic aggregate demand. We may, first, consider the case of an increase. If the economy is initially fully employed, countervailing deflationary measures are required. In many less developed countries, in which the export of materials weighs heavily, there is often much open or concealed unemployment, so that the expansionary effect of a rise in the world prices of important items in their exports is wholly to be welcomed; no countervailing measures are required. When there is on the overall average a drop in material prices, reflationary domestic measures will clearly be required.

Materials play only a minor part in U.K. exports; exports in this category play a somewhat greater part in U.S. exports, but still only quite a minor part in relation to the U.S. national income as a whole. It is mainly in the less developed countries that exports of materials play a major role. If there is a fall in the world price of an export, or of a group of exports, on which a less developed country is to an important extent dependent, it should reduce taxation. Yet again we have another paradox coughed up by economic dynamics. The maxim of the man in the street would probably be: 'This unfortunate country has had a nasty knock in respect of the commodity (or commodities) on the export of which it is largely dependent; so it had better economise in its own planning for the time being.' The opposite is the case. The reference here is to oscillations. Of course, if there has been a structural change, by which the goods made out of the material that the country supplies have gone permanently out of fashion, or if there has been an important invention of a prefabricated substitute, that is a different question; there will then be a long-range problem of what can be done for the country that has been thus badly hit.

But if it is a question only of oscillation, then an adversely affected country should reduce taxation. This reduction will entail its having a less favourable, or more unfavourable, external balance for the time being than it would otherwise have. This is yet another reason why the quantum of reserves available for international settlement should be increased above their present woefully inadequate level.

Some less developed countries seem to have had a wise intuition that they had a special need for good reserves, precisely to safeguard themselves against the evil consequences of a fall in the world prices for their special products. It is an interesting fact that, whereas the reserves of industrial countries increased by 14 per cent between 1962 and the second half of 1969, those of the less developed countries increased by 77 per cent. The second half of 1969, rather than 1970, is chosen for this illustration, because in the latter period the dollar crisis caused a supernormal increase in the (dollar) reserves of the industrial countries.

Nonetheless, it is probably not as yet an acknowledged maxim that a country hit by a fall in the world price or prices for goods figuring largely in its export receipts should reduce taxation. On the contrary, a country adopting such a policy might be in danger of getting a reputation for being irresponsible. Accordingly, it is vitally important that economic theorists, and economists in such institutions as the World Bank, should sedulously propagate the doctrine that, when prices of important items in the export bill fall, domestic taxation should be reduced. Countries complying with this doctrine would then be deemed to be conscientious, rather than irresponsible. This would influence capitalists in advanced countries in their judgement about whether it was wise to invest money in such or such a country.

Exports of finished manufactures may be expected to be confronted with a world income elasticity of demand in excess of one. By this means world prosperity is internationally propagated. The countries having a comparative advantage in producing goods on which a larger fraction of incremental world income than of total world income is spent will be at an advantage. So will those countries in the export domain of which technological progress is proceeding more rapidly than on the overall average.

An outline has been given of factors that influence the

growth rates of certain broad categories of imports and exports. The rate of growth of income is important; it divides into that due to the increase of population of working age and that due to the increase in its productivity. We then have to consider the income elasticity of the demand for the various items in the list of imports. In the case of items of goods wholly imported, the income elasticity of the demand for such imports will be simply the income elasticity of the demand for those goods. Portions of some items may be produced at home. Then all depends on whether the increase of domestic productivity of the items in question is greater or less than the increase of domestic productivity generally. If the two rates of increase are the same, we get an income elasticity of demand for imports of this type equal to the income elasticity of the demand for the products in question. If the rate of increase of domestic productivity in respect of these goods is less than the overall rate of increase of domestic productivity, the income elasticity of demand for imports of this class of goods will be greater than the income elasticity of demand for such goods, and conversely. In the case of goods subject to diminishing returns, like minerals, with growth the domestic supply of such goods may not be capable of proportionate increase, even if the technological improvements are as great in their case as those in the general domain, so that the income elasticity of the demand for imports of them will be greater than the overall income elasticity of the demand for them. The price elasticity of the import demand for food and basics may be expected to be low, and that for finished objects high.

As regards the trend of exports, what is happening to the increase of world demand, whether owing to population increase or productivity increase, is more important than what is happening at home, by comparison with what influences the trend of imports. Special note must be taken of what is happening in these respects in the areas to which a given country sends a proportion of its exports that is higher than the proportion of the incomes in such areas relatively to the world as a whole. Such a disproportionate distribution of exports may be due to geographical proximity or have historic causes, such as the 'British Empire'.

There is no reason to suppose that these various influences will have an equi-proportionate effect on the growth of the exports and on that of the imports of a given country. Thus there could be, and is most likely to be, a growing gap, one way or the other, in the trade balance of a particular country.

Similar considerations apply to 'invisible' items in the current account, such as tourism and foreign earnings (plus or minus) by advertisement. The question of capital movements will be dealt with in the next chapter.

If there is a growing improvement, or deterioration, in the current account – and it is surely probable that there will be one or the other – the consequence of this will impinge on the monetary authorities. In the case of fixed exchange rates an improvement will eventually entail a growth of the reserve of the monetary authority of the country in question; and conversely. If the policy is to secure adjustment by a change in the foreign exchange rate, then a rise in the growth rate of exports relatively to that of imports will require an upward adjustment of the exchange rate; and conversely. But this is subject to what has been said about price elasticities of demand.

An academic economist may use the expression 'and conversely' in this connection, as required by logic. But in the world of practical affairs, there is an a-symmetry at this point. There is a stiffer resistance to an upward valuation of a currency than there is to a devaluation. The motive for this is honourable; the responsible authorities in each country are reluctant to put its citizens to a disadvantage in world trade, such as is the inevitable result of an upward valuation; although a devaluation is bad for prestige, it helps industry to compete with foreigners, at home and abroad. In the modern world practical advantage is coming to be reckoned as more important than prestige. The Americans have, during the dollar crisis of 1971, been trying to get the best of two worlds, namely the advantage of a dollar devaluation without the loss of prestige associated with it. In a number of respects the Americans are, despite their bursting technological improvements, old-fashioned. And that is part of their charm.

Nonetheless, the fact that there is more resistance to an upward valuation than to a devaluation has to be considered in relation to the question of whether an adjustable exchange rate system is preferable to a fixed rate system. It can reasonably be held that the advantages of an adjustable system override the disadvantages of the a-symmetry. Let the countries with an upward trend in their balances of payments absorb some international reserve assets, while those with a downward trend devalue. That makes good enough sense; but there is a vitally important corallary. Under this system there would be a progressive accumulation of resources by the surplus countries. (Cf. the U.S.A. 1914–50.) This is but one among so many reasons, why it is vital that the sum total of media available to the central banks for holding as reserves should be made to grow.

Thus in the normal course of events, it is to be expected that some countries will have an improving balance on current account, while others have a worsening one. We may consider first the alternative of fixed exchange rates. In a country with a progressive increase in its balance of payments, the domestic money supply will rise, unless the authorities take counteracting measures, as they may well do. Accordingly it is more helpful to consider the case of countries with a declining external balance. This will lead to a decrease in the domestic money supply. If the reserve position of the country is very strong, as in the already cited case of the U.S.A. (1914–50), the authorities may offset this decrease by an open market policy designed to allow the domestic money supply to grow in the same proportion as the domestic natural growth rate of their country. More usually they will be inclined to allow the decrease in the money supply to eventuate, and even to reinforce it by open market operations.

By the old classical economics this would cause a decline of domestic prices and thereby lead to an improvement in the country's balance of payments, proceeding until equilibrium in it was restored. But, according to Keynesian thinking, the deflationary measures taken by the authorities on such an occasion are likely to have a more powerful effect in increasing unemployment than in depressing supply prices. And so we are back to the dilemma already discussed. Do we want an international monetary system, by the regular working of which a substantial amount of unemployment may be created from time to time, and almost certainly will be, since it is most unlikely that the factors that have been specified as influencing the growth of imports and exports respectively will cause an equal balance of payments? The effect of deflationary measures on activity, which Keynes believed to be more important than their effect on prices, will doubtless in due course have the effect of restoring to equilibrium the country's external balance of payments. But is this the best way to achieve this desirable, and in the long run, necessary, result?

Alternatively, the external balance can be redressed by a downward adjustment of the foreign exchange rate. This has the advantage that it does not necessarily involve a decline in domestic activity, or an increase of unemployment. But, as against this, it may not achieve what is required. For success, it is needful that the elasticities of supply and demand for the country's exports and imports should be sufficient. But this is a doubtful matter. By contrast, domestic deflation can be relied on with certainty to restore equilibrium in the balance of payments. This is because it operates on activity and real income, and, if the reduction in these goes far enough, the demand for imports, as governed by income elasticity, will also go far enough to restore external equilibrium. But this system is objectionable, because the certainty of its success depends on its power to create a great evil – unemployment.

And so, within the range of what has been considered, we have a choice between a system (fixed exchange rates) that can be relied on to produce the needed effect, but at the price of the great evil of unemployment, the dimensions of which will be determined by the circumstances of the case, and an alternative system (flexible exchange rates) that cannot be relied on to produce the needed effect. If a country that is operating a flexible exchange rate system finds that a devaluation does not produce an equal balance of external payments, it will doubtless reinforce its curative endeavours by domestic deflation, which will reduce the quantum of domestic activity and thereby of imports by a sufficient amount. If it is unwilling to do this, it will have to resort to some other method, like import restrictions, for restoring its external balance.

It will be needful in due course to reassess the importance of targets. The avoidance of unemployment, apart from frictional, has surely top priority. By comparison with that the loss of benefit owing to some restrictions on the freedom of international trade is likely to be trivial. But that does not seem to be the view of those at present in high places.

9 International Capital Movements

As a broad generalisation it is usually laid down that capital tends to flow from the advanced and well-endowed countries to the needy ones. This is not a proposition of universal validity. For instance, in certain years there have been net inflows of capital into the U.S.A., the best endowed of all countries. And the distribution of outflowing capital is not always in favour of the most needy; for instance there has been a recent tendency for more American capital to go to the well-endowed countries of Europe than to the less developed countries.

There are three fundamental factors governing the general trend. We shall deal in the first instance with direct rather than portfolio investment. (i) The ratio of resource allocation that can profitably be devoted to capital formation to national income may be higher than the ratio of domestic saving to national income in less developed countries: while the reverse may be the case in the mature countries. The former may be regarded as undersaving countries, and, if the latter are over-saving, it is natural that there should be a flow from the one set to the other.

(ii) Capital formation has in the past usually been more heavily dependent on technological know-how than has the production of consumer goods. The provision of capital disposal for direct investment in foreign countries has tended to be linked with the provision of the relevant technological know-how. The richer countries are more heavily endowed with this than the poorer countries.

(iii) The latter are apt to lack efficient capital markets, whereby the savings of the general run of persons in the country can be made accessible for those needing capital disposal to initiate real capital formation. There may be savings in principle available for the development of the country that are not used for that purpose, since there is no channel through which they can flow. Entrepreneurs in advanced countries, who spot profitable opportunities for direct investment abroad will probably have no great difficulty in raising funds in their own domestic capital markets.

Classical doctrine postulates that there will be such international flows of capital as are required to secure that the profit on marginal ventures in each country is the same in all countries. This should be secured by private enterprise. This is, however, subject to the estimation on the part of entrepreneurs investing abroad that they incur greater risk in doing so; on this basis the profit rate would be expected to be lower in countries from which there is a net outflow of capital than in countries having a net inflow. There are two aspects of the greater risk. One is that the entrepreneur may have less knowledge about all the details affecting productive establishments abroad than he has about those at home and may accordingly be more likely to make mistakes in relation to his foreign ventures. The other is that in many cases he may have less confidence in the stability of the political regimes abroad, and therefore greater fear that his capital may be lost by outright confiscation or a breakdown of orderly conditions *in situ*. This lack of confidence may be well founded. Nonetheless, on balance it is probable that these risk factors, in part psychological only, reduce the international flow of capital below the optimum level.

There are, however, also factors working in the opposite direction. There may be what is known as 'exploitation' in some countries, notably the less developed. By the older orthodoxy the market will secure that the wages of labour are equal to its marginal product. More recently we had embodied in orthodox statics the doctrines of imperfect competition. In the absence of a perfect labour market, the value of the marginal product of a unit of labour will tend to be equated, not to the wage of that unit, but to the 'marginal outlay' on it. If the value of the marginal product of labour is rising, it will not necessarily pay the employer to raise wages accordingly. It is the function of trade unions to see that he does so. But, where trade unions are weak, or non-existent, exploitation may occur, and profit be swollen thereby. From the point of view of the optimum distribution of the use of capital, profit should be reckoned net of any element in it due to exploitation. Capital may go abroad to take advantage of the existence of 'cheap' labour there. 'Cheap' in this context does not refer to a wage that is low because the labour is correspondingly inefficient, but only to one that is below the level that would correspond to its inefficiency. Thus an international equality of profit as between countries where there are unequal degrees of exploitation would not get an optimum distribution. It may be counter-argued that an inflow of capital into a country of exploitation would probably cause the labour there to do better than it otherwise would, and therefore, while not securing the maximum output of goods in the world, would be beneficial by getting a better world distribution of the goods.

So far this chapter has been concerned with static economics. We have to consider growth. Should we expect the amount of capital formation, conceived on the best estimate of what is likely to be profitable, to grow at the same rate as national income? If the capital-intensity of the methods of production of incremental income remains the same, the two growth rates would be the same. In advanced countries the growth rate in the required amount of new capital might well be lower than that of income owing to the tendency to devote a rising fraction of income to the purchase of services. Then there is the question of whether current technological inventions are becoming more (or less) capital-intensive. There is a difference in the case of the less developed countries, importing foreign know-how. In advanced countries – perhaps one ought to say in the most advanced country of all, the U.S.A.! – the nature of the current technological progress depends on new knowledge forthcoming on the frontiers of applied science. Less developed countries will largely be incorporating into their production systems technological methods already well-known elsewhere. It is likely that these more sophisticated methods will be more capital-intensive than the more primitive methods hitherto used, and, if growing amounts are introduced, capital formation will grow more quickly than national income. Foreign skills are in the process of being applied to their production. This relates not only to items purchased by citizens with their incremental income, but also to replacements: the same old goods will be produced in a new and more capital-intensive way.

It may well be that, in a certain phase of development, the

capital-intensity of increments of output will be represented by a humped curve. This is the phase in which the creation of infrastructure plays an especially important part, namely when we move from a primitive to a modern set-up. One thinks of the building of railways, the provision of electricity, irrigation. Doubtless the creation of infrastructure will continue to be an important part of the increment of output, but not so much so as during the transition from primitive to modern methods of transport, etc.

To the extent that income growth is lower in one country than another, capital requirements will *ceteris paribus* be a smaller fraction of current income – the desired saving ratio being a still smaller fraction. Meanwhile there will probably be a rise in the desired saving ratio, if income increases. To the extent that this is not offset by a diminished capital inflow, it will raise the warranted growth rate. At the same time capital markets may improve, so that an increased proportion of what saving there is enters into the productive system, instead of being waylaid in the purchase of gold and precious stones. These factors would make the countries less dependent on the outside world for the achievement of their optimum ('natural') growth rates. On the other hand, in less developed countries the need for imported know-how is likely to rise more than aggregate income, since manufactures will constitute a rising proportion of increments of income.

Some elements in the growth of capital requirements have been roughly sketched. In the last chapter the growth of some broad categories of imports and exports were also roughly sketched. In that chapter it seemed that it would be only by a happy coincidence if exports and imports grew at the same rate, except if influenced by specific governmental or central bank policies designed to make them balance. If we superimpose on the picture there given the kind of forces that govern the motives or requirements for international capital movements, do we get a summation that leads to the outcome of a continuance of an equal basic balance of external payments?

A word should be said about portfolio investment. The processes that occur in national stock exchanges slop over, so to speak, into the international arena. The flows in a national stock exchange do not consist only of the investment of fresh savings in the securities offered there. Far more important are the continuous shiftings of funds from one security to another, and, as a result of supply and demand forces, continuous revaluations of the various securities. The tendency is for the relation between the best estimated, or guessed, future dividends of a firm, perhaps rising through time, and the current value of its securities to be the same for firms of equal reputed reliability. There will be a spectrum of reliabilities and a corresponding spectrum of the relations between estimated future profit and the current value of the securities. The consequent value of a firm's shares has no direct relation to the value of its assets, whether these are valued at historic costs or at replacement costs, minus its liabilities.

This process of shifting in such a way as to establish the aforementioned equalities may extend into the international sphere. Judgements about the prospects and reliability of firms may differ from country to country. The international flows of portfolio capital will mainly relate to the securities of large firms, since judgements about the reliability of small foreign firms cannot be so well based. This is analogous to the impediment to direct investment overseas, constituted by the lack of knowledge of detailed circumstances there.

Net portfolio investment in long-term foreign securities is included in long-term capital outflow; and conversely. And this is quite proper. Accordingly, such investment is included in the 'basic balance'.

At first glance it might be thought that, since the foreign world is a bigger place than the home country, the amount of portfolio investment outflowing from a particular country would normally be greater than that inflowing. This is clearly a fallacy, since in the aggregate inflows must equal outflows on any particular account in the world as a whole. Portfolio investments flowing out of a particular country must land up somewhere, and constitute an inflow there. The correct statement is that there will be a net outflow from countries in which the ratio of the weight of increasing investment opportunities, given by home-based companies of rising prospects and reliability, to national saving, is less than the ratio of the weight of increasing investment opportunities given by all companies in the world to world saving; and conversely.

The international flow of portfolio capital is regularly, and rightly, included in the calculation of the basic balances of the various particular countries. Does this make it seem likely that the basic balance will normally tend to equality?

The expression 'basic balance', as commonly used, is defined as constituted by the current account together with long-term capital movements. The concept of basic balance that we need for this analysis should include some movements of short-term capital also, namely those that, so to speak, follow in the train of trade and long-term direct investment. A parent firm may lend a subsidiary abroad some working capital; traders may need to have liquid funds in the various centres where they do business. Doubtless each individual one of these balances goes up and down from time to time. But, if the overall aggregate of such balances lent by residents of country A to operators in country B rises year by year, the increment should be included in the concept of the 'basic balance', as needed for our purposes.

There are other short-term capital movements, which should not be included within the basic balance. Those divide into the helpful and perverse. The helpful are those that offset seasonal variations in payments or other temporary dislocations. They are due to be reversed in due course. They may be motivated by the current level of exchange rates, *assuming fixed parities*; a trader, for instance, foreseeing the need for sterling at a future date may take advantage of the quotation for sterling being currently low, within the fixed limits, and buy it at once, spot or forward. When in due course he meets his commitment, this short-term loan to the U.K. is paid off.

Within the broad category of helpful movements should normally be included transfers of liquid funds designed to take advantage of differentials in short-term interest rates as between different countries. The Bank of England may put up the Bank Rate, precisely in order to attract short term funds for the time being. A movement into the U.K. of such funds should clearly not be included in the basic balance of the U.K.; on the contrary it is the method by which a temporary imbalance of the U.K. is financed. From the point of view of the Bank of England, this movement of funds is clearly helpful. Of course there may be other countries that are furious with the Bank of England for putting up its Bank Rate at a particular juncture, and deem the consequent movement of funds into the U.K. as decidedly unhelpful. This would be a symptom of the continuing lack of consensus among countries about what the appropriate measures are to deal with specific problems as they arise.

There is a more serious point. The Bank of England may have put up the Bank Rate, not in order to attract foreign funds, but to deal with certain domestic problems, and it may be embarrassed by the inflow of funds. In such a case the international capital movement would be unhelpful to all parties. This brings us to the deeper problems of the adequacy of available weapons to achieve all targets of policy, of the lack of a well-grounded and agreed theory about the proper use of the weapons that there are, and, underlying that, the imperfect condition of economic dynamics itself.

The most notable instances of unhelpful movements of short-term capital are purchases of a currency because the purchasers believe that the currency in question will in due course be valued upwards and sales of a currency because it is believed that it will be valued downwards. In some cases these beliefs may be true. And that again divides into two parts. It may be the case that the currency in question really ought to be revalued in due course and would in any event be revalued. Some might even go so far as to think that such anticipatory movements of funds are helpful by jogging the laggard authorities into acting more promptly; that, however, is not acceptable; a proper system must be managed by those responsible for it; they must not be pushed around by irresponsible outsiders. The other case is where the revaluation is not required by any basic disequilibrium, but is forced on the authorities by the movements of funds themselves, which may be very massive. A sub-class of this case is when some revaluation is intended and correct, but on execution is made larger than it ought to be by the relevant criteria, in order to convince the world that it will not shortly have to be followed by another revaluation in the same direction. All such movements of funds are injurious. Of course they are not to be included in the estimation of the basic balance of the country in question.

Movements of short-term capital in anticipation of probable or possible exchange rate changes are often referred to as 'speculative'. Although there may be some speculative movements, especially when the situation is boiling up into a crisis, it is to be stressed that by far the greater part of these movements are not speculative, but precautionary, being made at the instance of highly conscientious and well-intentioned advisers, seeking to protect those, who consult or employ them, from loss. Nothing could be further from the truth than to impute a malign motive to them. It is true that the effect of these movements may be injurious. That is not the fault of the advisers, but of the system itself.

It would doubtless be very difficult from a statistical point of view to establish what part of the short-term capital movements occurring in normal times ought properly to be included in the 'basic balance' and what part is the consequence of an imbalance.

After the inclusion of such part of short-term capital movements as ought to be included in the basic balance, it is still not clear that the various and diverse causes at work will tend to cause an equal balance or even a movement towards one.

What then happens? With fixed exchange rates, reserves will rise or fall according to the circumstances. With adjustable or floating rates, these rates will change. We may take the former alternative.

If the basic balance is favourable, reserves will tend to increase, and the domestic money supply will also increase by an equal absolute amount. The authorities may choose to offset this, having their eyes on the domestic situation. In this case the external balance will continue to improve. Alternatively they may choose to permit the increase in the money supply to occur and indeed to supplement the increase sufficiently to maintain the pre-existing ratio between the money supply and reserves. This would be appropriate as a move towards bringing the external balance of payments towards equality.

If there is initially unemployment, as there may well be, all will work in happy harmony. Easy money will increase domestic activity and at the same time make the external balance tend towards equality. This will happen both on trade and long-term capital accounts. Easy money will have some influence, although not a proportionate one, in lowering the yields of long-term domestic assets and thereby make investors look around the world for something better.

But if there is initially full employment – and there is no reason why there should not be – easier money will tend to cause demand-pull inflation. Accordingly, the authorities may be hesitant to adopt such a policy. So, what will they do in relation to the external imbalance? Perhaps nothing. Countries in adverse balance have not this happy liberty of choice.

In their case it will be needful not to offset the decline in the money supply, or even possibly needful to re-enforce it. If initially a demand-pull inflation is proceeding, this will be to the good, from both points of view. But, if initially there is under-employment, or, even, just full employment, tight money will tend to cause unemployment. So, there is a conflict.

Professor Mundell has proposed that we should break away from the system of having two horses harnessed to the same carriage, namely monetary and fiscal policies, by which both are simultaneously either whipped on or reined in. You cannot in these circumstances whip one horse on, while reining in the other. Instead, he proposes that fiscal policy should be geared to maintaining full employment, but avoiding demand-pull inflation domestically, while monetary policy should be used for securing an equal external balance. This seems to entail that the external balance is maintained in equality by an appropriate capital movement in or out of the country, as influenced by monetary policy – that is by the level of interest rates. If a high interest rate tended to damp domestic activity, this would under his system be offset by pressing the foot harder on the fiscal accelerator; and conversely. This scheme would not correct the external balance on trade account, since his fiscal policy would maintain domestic activity at full employment level and thus cause no abatement in the demand for imports and would have no effect on wage-price spiralling if that were proceeding. Accordingly for the external balance it relies wholly on the influence of domestic monetary policy on the inflow or outflow of capital.

There are two troubles about this. One is that some countries, notably the less developed, do not have sufficiently well organised markets for capital of long or short term for 'monetary policy' to avail in attracting capital to or repelling it from the country.

The other is that it assumes that it is legitimate to tailor capital movements in or out of the country to the state of its current account balance. Is this a proper assumption?

This question takes us on to wider terrain. If monetary and fiscal policies cannot by themselves avail to achieve both domestic full employment and an equal external balance, and if flexible exchange rates cannot by themselves secure a rectification on an external balance owing to insufficient elasticities of home demand for inputs and foreign demand for domestic products, and also if their use is limited by practical difficulties, we may be driven to contemplate some direct interference with the free international flow of trade or capital.

When this possibility is envisaged, it is widely assumed that a restriction of international capital movements would be preferable to a restriction on trade. *Why?* What is the logic behind this lower priority for the freedom of capital movements? To judge from the writings of experts it appears to be just a dogma, like those enforced by the Inquisition.

In my own opinion there is an optimum international capital flow which is not always, or even usually, identical with that which would occur under freedom of international capital movement, as I shall presently explain. (But are there not also some acknowledged limitations on the absolute freedom of trade, from the infant industry argument, as propounded by Hamilton and List and endorsed by that great Free Trader, J.S. Mill, onwards?) To hold that, in order to get the optimum international flow of capital one may have to impose restrictions (or, possibly, give subsidies), is something entirely different from holding that capital flows should be tailored, in order to get an equal overall balance, leaving trade completely free. One would think that, if welfare is indeed increased by a given capital flow, the quantum of such benefit would be likely to be greater than that lost by a marginal paring down of international trade.

In the Articles of Agreement of the I.M.F. freedom of trade is given priority over freedom of capital movement. This may have been due in part to the influence of Keynes – I have no direct evidence on this point. Keynes had long been hostile to international investment as such. He was deeply suspicious of the American plan for what has eventuated in the World

Bank.[1] It was only on the ship taking him to the Bretton Woods conference that he relaxed his attitude, and then, in true Keynesian style, he made a memorable advocacy of it at the preliminary conference in Atlantic City.

When in the sixties the U.S.A. had experienced protracted difficulties with its balance of payments, it enacted the Interest Equalization Tax on a section of its capital exports; later President Johnson initiated a voluntary, and, subsequently, mandatory, restraint. Why was not some restriction of imports considered first? Of course, if, by some criteria, the U.S.A. was exporting too much capital from an optimum welfare standpoint, there should have been restrictions, whether there was an overall deficit or not. The question whether, if there has to be restriction, it should be imposed first on capital movement or on trade should be regarded as an open one, to be decided on the merits of the case.

This brings us to a very fundamental point. In pure growth theory I have stressed that the basic axioms should relate to the mutual consistency of the various growth rates at a particular point of time. These rates are governed by certain fundamental determinants, including prospects as best estimated at that point of time. Of course unexpected events of significant importance may happen, indeed are continually happening. These, when they occur, lead to the need for revised assessments of the values of the fundamental determinants and of the various growth rates. The concept of a steady growth rate implies a backward as well as a forward look. If there have been inflections in the past, within the relevant time horizon, this will cause present growth rates to be different from what they would be, if they were governed only by the fundamental determinants currently operating.

When in this context we come to the external balance of payments, investment in foreign countries should be regarded as a *favourable* item in the external balance of payments. This is in contrast with static analysis, where we take net current capital outflow to be an unfavourable item, while at the same time recording, in another part of the table, net interest and

---

[1] I recall Harry White asking me to use what influence I might have with Keynes to try to make him more sympathetic. But I do not recall that I did so.

dividends on past foreign investment as a favourable item. If in a given year a country stopped investing abroad, its basic balance would be better than it would be if it continued to invest. In dynamics we have to have regard in that particular year to a continuing process. In a ten-year period – it might be somewhat longer, but is probably shorter – the interest and profit on foreign investment overtop the capital outlay. Thus a country that regularly invests £200 million abroad, or, rather an amount rising each year at a regular rate, will have a more favourable balance of external payments than one which invests £100 million a year only. Similarly, amounts borrowed from abroad should be regarded as an adverse item. Less developed countries that have balance of payments problems are absolutely in the right if they are unwelcome to foreign capital.

In statics one is accustomed to the distinction between a short-period effect and a long-period effect. That distinction disappears in dynamics, because there we are concerned with a continuing process. Long-period effects are currently occurring.

The American experience gives a good illustration of capital export being a favourable item in an external balance of payments:

	1950	1970
	Million dollars	
(i) Interest and profit on foreign investment	1593	9601
(ii) Capital export	1265	6529
(iii) Excess of (i) over (ii) (net effect on basic balance)	+328	+3072

It is clear that the role of the U.S.A. as an exporter of capital was a factor tending to improve its external balance of payments; this is in line with what economic analysis would lead one to expect. Yet after long-drawn-out deficits, Presidents Kennedy and Johnson both thought that a correct rectifying measure was to curb capital exports. The curbs did not actually suffice to cure the trouble of the U.S. external balance in the short term; this is not the place to analyse the complex problems involved as regards the continuing U.S. deficits; but it is likely that even as early as 1971, the U.S. balance of payments would have been better, had the Kennedy–Johnson curbs on capital exports not been imposed. It is rather suprising that in the nineteen-sixties, the richest and most sophisticated country in the world should have thought it appropriate to have regard to the short period only in dealing with its external deficits. It took measures that were temporarily helpful, but bound to be adverse in the long run. So does the richest and most sophisticated country in the world still, right up to our own day, have its eyes glued to the current situation only, in its external balance of payments? Does it, in fact, have cognisance only of economic statics and not of economic dynamics? It may be, it is true, that there are some countries that are more sophisticated, although much poorer than the U.S.A., such as India. Some attribute their lack of welcome to the inflow of foreign capital to nationalism – there may be something in that; but they also have the understanding that an inflow of foreign capital will exacerbate their external balance of payments problem. This is not to imply that the Indians have better brain power than the Americans, although it is possible that they have; the point is that poverty sharpens the wits.

At the time of the Kennedy–Johnson measures the Americans had been running external deficits for a substantial period, viz. since late 1957. It was time to take remedial action. But when such action is eventually taken, it should surely be addressed to having its effect in the long run, rather than immediately. It would be counter-argued by some that the Americans were obliged to do something that had a quick effect, since their reserves were all too rapidly seeping away. This takes us back to the need for greater reserves of media for international settlement. World reserves in ratio to trade had fallen by 1969 to less than a third of their pre-war level, which was not at that time considered excessive. (They have grown towards 40 per cent since then, still a very low figure, to a minor extent owing to the issuance of S.D.Rs, but to a major extent to a turning in of dollars by private holders to the various central banks, owing to a rising distrust, well justified, as it proved to be, in dollars.)

Owing to the operation of chance causes, some time often has to elapse before a continuing deficit (or excessive surplus) can be taken as a sure signal that fundamental measures ought to be adopted to eliminate it. If a country is in fundamental deficit, and if the authorities think that the appropriate way of remedying it is to influence capital flow rather than the trade flow, then the measure adopted should be such as to *encourage capital outflow*. Conjugated with a greater capital outflow is an improved external balance of payments. It is true that if there is an inflection at a certain point of time, in the period immediately following that point an increased capital outflow will cause a deterioration in the balance. But, when the authorities see fit to change the fundamental determinants, they should have their eyes fixed on growth rates – of exports, imports, earnings of capital, etc. – and not on the immediate short-term static effects. Accordingly, when a country, experiencing sustained external deficit, decides that it is appropriate to find a remedy by operating on the capital flow, namely by increasing the outflow, it must have enough reserves to tide over the, say, ten-year period, during which the increased outflow worsens the basic balance, pending its ultimate effect in improving that balance.

It has been argued above that, given the right time horizon and a sufficiency of reserves, the Americans ought, from the point of view of their own external balance of payments – a problem still (1971) unsolved – to have encouraged a higher level of annual overseas investment by the Americans. It does not follow that such an encouragement would have been beneficial to welfare in the world as a whole. This depends on wider considerations.

By analogous reasoning potential importers of foreign capital, especially the less developed countries, would in many cases be wise to be unwelcome to it. This does not apply to the oil producers, who have a high and rising external trade balance. They may anticipate being easily able to cover the increasing toll of profits to be remitted abroad out of their still more strongly rising trade balance, owing to the increasing exports of oil. There may have to be a 'Caution' sign for countries whose oil supply is in danger of running dry; but oil supplies seldom seem to run dry.

The U.K. in the period between 1850 and the outbreak of the First World War was an exceptional instance of benign harmony, and it would be wrong for others to regard its experience as a precedent, as was often pointed out by Hubert Henderson. Its exports of capital were high and increasing, until by 1914 they neared the figure of 10 per cent of national income. I believe this to be easily an all-time world record; it is certainly far above anything that the Americans have more recently achieved. Nonetheless the proceeds of the investments rose more rapidly than the investments themselves. At the same time there was a rapid increase of population in Britain and a strong rise in productivity per person; this must be taken in conjunction with diminishing returns in domestic food production in a small island and the fact that the main part of the population, still extremely poor in 1850, spent a high proportion of its increase of income on food. Accordingly, food imports rose rapidly. Productivity in British domestic agriculture increased considerably in this period, although not as rapidly as it has done since the Second World War, and by no means sufficiently to meet the growing requirements of the domestic population for food. Thus there was a balance between rising revenue due to foreign investments (exceeding the growing annual amount of investment abroad) and sharply increasing needs for imports. On the other side of the blanket, the U.K. investments were largely in the U.S.A. and the Argentine, both big food exporters, so that they could cover their increasing net bill on capital account by their rising exports to the U.K. There was also considerable capital export to continental Europe. Export of capital to the British Commonwealth came rather later, but there was still a happy harmony, since the Commonwealth came to supply a rising proportion of British food imports. It must not be assumed that there will normally be such a happy harmony between a rich country with capital available for export and the regular trend of its import requirements. At a later date there might have been a rift in the harmony unfavourable to the outside world, if Britain had not had to sell so many foreign investments to finance two world wars.

The import of capital into an undersaving country may increase national income after subtracting what has to be paid to the foreign capitalists by way of interest and dividends; indeed one would expect that normally to be so. But the balance of external payments also has to be looked at. For a country with a handsome and possibly rising surplus on trade account (cf. the oil states cited above) there is no problem. But not all undersaving countries are in this condition. Some, if welcoming foreign capital, may have to devote a rising fraction of their output to securing a better external trade balance. What motives operate on producers and traders to secure the result? According to old-fashioned doctrine the authorities should furnish a motive by domestic deflation, namely a reduction of domestic demand, causing potential exporters to look around the outside world for markets for their surpluses and causing citizens, with their lower post-deflation incomes, to import less. Then one has to raise the question whether the net increase of domestic income, due to the foreign capital flowing in, is greater or less than the loss of income due to diminished domestic employment. There is no *a priori* answer to the question; empirical research is needed.

A more modern orthodoxy prescribes devaluation as the best method for improving the external trade balance. This usually entails a loss, owing to worsened terms of trade. Again there is the empirical problem of assessing the amount of this loss by comparison with the production gain due to the capital inflow. The likelihood of net loss is larger, the larger the proportion of the country's output that is sold abroad. All depends on elasticities of supply and demand. In the case when a country's exports consist largely of raw materials or food, having world prices, the elasticity of foreign demand may sometimes be almost infinite, but the elasticity of supply may be low; a rise in the domestic price may not enable producers to raise their output much. The elasticity of foreign demand will not be so high when the country in question is an important supplier, within the world scene, of a commodity that bulks large in its export bill. The price elasticity of its demand for imports may be low, to the extent that these consist of capital goods not producible at home, or for consumer goods, which people rising out of a subsistence level regard as 'necessities' at the next higher level of income, perhaps also not producible at home. The fact has to be faced that the devaluation may in cases not improve the external balance of payments. What then? Exports can be subsidised and this has proved useful in some cases, e.g. in Latin America, but it is not very useful if the elasticity of supply is low. The most sensible remedy may be the one very widely adopted, although frowned upon, namely to impose direct restrictions on imports.

It is a question of balancing the loss due to the marginal benefits of participation in the international division of labour against that due (on the devaluation remedy) to worsened terms of trade. And behind that there is the question of balancing the loss due to either of these procedures against the loss that would result from a restriction of foreign capital imports and the consequent loss of domestic production.

The question may then be asked – why cannot the capital importing countries do their own saving as needed for development at the maximum feasible rate? Once again, the answer falls into two parts. (i) There is the painfulness of increased saving in a poor country. (ii) The imported capital is usually linked with know-how. The poor countries could at a pinch provide themselves with more saving; but they could not, on their own, provide themselves with the extra know-how that imported capital often brings with it.

If any economy has achieved steady growth at the natural rate, saving presents no problem. At each round a certain fraction of the increment of income is saved, so that income and capital grow in harmony. The minimum acceptable rate of return is governed by the formula for the optimum rate of interest, as set out on p. 80. This in turn will govern the degree of capital intensity of the methods of production chosen. The natural growth is limited by the maximum feasible rate of expansion of qualified personnel including that of skilled entrepreneurship. Appropriate know-how may be a bottleneck; it may be possible to import some. An important factor limiting natural growth may be uncertainty about the future. In a less developed country, where a high proportion of the population is working at a subsistence level, the spatial horizons may be too narrow for them to embark on lines of production that would otherwise be feasible; marketing and transport arrangements may be quite inadequate.

Then something may happen to cause a breakthrough. It might be a political revolution, or, more moderately, the accession to governmental power of persons determined to get things moving. This would entail an inflection in the growth curve. During the inflection – or we should say in the period following it – capital requirements may be abnormally high. To get a matching amount of saving, it may be needful to reduce consumption. In a normal advance saving, as required, is found by people setting aside a certain fraction of their incomes; they will set aside a given fraction of their continuing income and of their increments of income. In this condition there will be no need to reduce spending; on the contrary spending will rise, since people will save a fraction only of their increments of income; the rest of the increments are available for increased spending. Thus the growth of consumption and of capital can proceed simultaneously in harmony. But when there is an upward inflection in the rate of advance, the formula for the optimum saving ratio, may, for the time, entail a reduction of consumption.

The idea of a cutback in consumption has to be looked at rather closely. There may be an asymmetry in the diminishing utility of income curve. We may consider incomes of £x and £x + 1 respectively. Someone may at a given point be enjoying an income of £x and contemplate with satisfaction its prospective increase to £x + 1. That satisfaction is what we call the marginal utility of income. But let the person already be enjoying an income of £x + 1 and be told that it is about to be cut down to £x only. The displeasure caused by such a prospect may be much greater than the pleasure that was at a previous date caused by the rise of income from £x to £x + 1. The prospect of having better food and clothes is very nice; if the person was told that the increment would have to be cut down, or postponed, he would not be, so to speak, heartbroken. But if, having enjoyed a better standard for some years, he is told that he will have to go back to the poorer diet and shabbier clothes of previous times, that will vex him very much indeed.

In this notable work, entitled *Introduction to the Theory of Growth in a Socialist Economy*, Michal Kalecki discusses the problem.[1] He makes no use of the concept of utility of income. This is – can we meaningfully say 'was' instead of 'is'? – precluded by socialist ideology. To take its place, he uses the concept of a government decision curve. The extent to which current consumption is to be sacrificed for the sake of higher growth is to be determined by the arbitrary decisions of the

[1] See also p. 30 above.

central government. He postulates that the Government would not activate capital development at a rate that actually caused a temporary decline in consumption, and, further, that in the interim period it would (should?) hold capital development down to a level that made possible some increase in consumption, although not so great a one as would occur, if there was no stepping up of capital formation. His argument is in terms of a self-dependent economy.

May capital inflow into less developed countries serve to ease this problem? There are two considerations working in opposite directions. On the one hand the import of foreign capital must be regarded as a negative item in the balance of payments. For all countries having an actual or prospective adverse balance, this consideration must weigh heavily. The various methods of correcting the external balance are likely to reduce the growth of income below what would otherwise be its potential. On the other hand foreign capital may raise the level of domestic capital formation above the level that could be achieved without temporarily depressing living standards in the recipient countries.

The former consideration should be more heavily stressed, because it is much less in the minds of economic experts and commentators. Countries, and, of course, especially less developed countries, should be most wary about the amount of foreign capital that they allow in, unless they have an easy and maintainable, preferably growing, surplus on their external trade account. Advanced country interpreters tend to regard restrictions by developing countries as symptoms of nationalism; it is likely that in most cases they are actuated by wise economic judgement. Less developed countries should be very chary indeed about the amount of foreign capital that they allow to flow in. Some modicum may be allowed in the transition from a subsistence economy, especially to help with infrastructure. It should be understood that permissiveness should be for moderate amounts only and having a fairly short time limit. Some firms, including multinational corporations, start investing in less developed countries, with a view to expanding their operations in due course. In the face of these, the countries concerned should exhibit a placard clearly inscribed with the letters NO.

What the less developed nations above all require is an

increase of know-how. Foreign capital brings this with it and deploys it in their territories. And this is to their advantage. Indeed the import of know-how is what they most need. It might be a good idea for the less developeds to have a law, by which they would allow foreign capital to come in, only on condition that all know-how involved in its operations in them, whether deployed in the less developed countries concerned or in the home countries from which the capital originated, should be made available to potential domestic producers, whether to all and sundry or only to those getting a certificate from the government.

'Aid' is of course wholly to be welcomed. So probably are interest-free loans, provided that the redemption date is far ahead. This depends on a country's balance of payments. Twenty years is rather a short period. Low-interest loans should be regarded with great scepticism, especially when they are low only relatively to very high rates (by historic standards) currently prevailing. To draw a bow at a venture, I would suggest 2 per cent as the maximum interest rate that should be regarded as 'low'. From the point of view of the burdensomeness on developing countries of foreign borrowing, the relation of the interest charged by international or national agencies designed to help less developed countries, to the current level of world interest rates is irrelevant.

'Do-gooders' in thought or action have, and have had, some influence on what the philistines in power actually do. It is accordingly most important that their ideas should be governed by accurate, and not by sloppy, thinking. They appear on the whole to believe that it is a splendid thing for the rich countries to make large direct investments in or loans to the less developeds. Advanced countries vie with each other in attracting the attention of the good-doers to what they have been doing in these respects. The do-gooders do not appreciate that capital investment in less developed countries above a certain limited amount may do long-run damage to their interests. The heretic, Karl Marx, understood this rather well.

What the do-gooders should concentrate their attention on is the distribution of know-how to countries relatively short of it. Something may seep out from the activities of multinational corporations or other direct investors to the native population.

I am not able to assess the quantitative importance of this; I am sure that this conveyance of know-how is much less than the recipient countries need for their own optimum development. The do-gooders should strongly press upon do-gooding international or national agencies to provide for the distribution of know-how on a *large* scale to those who need it. This could be done to some extent from the staffs available to the agencies; but more important would be big subsidies on the export of know-how.

Of course know-how can be bought. Here we come to another instance of 'conflict'. Conveyors of know-how to less developed countries have to stay for some time in those countries, to set things going. Actually they usually stay for too short a time. They are paid salaries in accordance with the structure of salaries in their home countries. And these are often many times as much as the salaries of equivalent native personnel. The latter may have been trained in technology at places of the highest repute in America or Europe and have just as good brain power as the visiting purveyors of know-how. But there are not, and cannot be, enough of them. This creates discord, and, indeed, a reluctance by some less developed countries to invite foreign purveyors of know-how. I suggest that top priority should be given to schemes whereby international or national do-gooding agencies regularly subvented the incomes of foreign experts advising less developed countries. Thus the governments or firms in these countries could pay the foreign experts at the same rates as those applying to equivalent native experts; the foreign experts would have their pay topped up by the international agencies. Of course those 'in the know' would realise that this was being done, but not the general run of people; furthermore the actual deterrent for domestic firms to employing foreign experts would be eliminated.

The subsidisation of the export of know-how from the advanced to the less developed countries is by far the most important thing that can be done to help them. And the flow of know-how should be independent of the flow of capital, the optimum level of which is governed by quite different considerations.

On balance the trend of this chapter has been rather unfavourable to the international movement of capital. I hold that some restriction is desirable. But that is entirely different from the view that the flow of capital should be tailored by restrictions, so as to get an overall equal basic balance of external payments, having regard to a possible imbalance on the current account.

Keynes was prevailingly hostile to foreign investment. As I have described, it was only in his voyage to Bretton Woods that he was convinced that the World Bank was a good idea. But the promotion of the World Bank, with all its criteria for assessing benefit, was something quite different from allowing a free international flow of private capital. However, the motives for his hostility were rather different from mine. He looked at the matter mainly from the selfish point of view of the investing country, especially the U.K. He stressed the importance of default, and, by statistical research over a long period, claimed to show that the net return on British foreign investment was way below the return on investment at home. Accordingly let us discourage foreign investment. Intertwined with this idea was the idea that it was desirable to encourage domestic investment, so as to reduce unemployment here, which was so high during the period of his most active thinking on this subject. Defaults on foreign investment do not seem to have been so great since 1945 as they were during the period reviewed by Keynes.

In my view there should be restrictions on international capital in accordance with the criteria that I have striven to define, albeit only roughly, in this chapter. These criteria should establish an optimum rate of capital outflow (or inflow). Given that optimum, I hold that there should be much greater reluctance to disturb capital movement in accordance with it than to impose restrictions on the freedom of trade, when traditional weapons seem unable to secure the appropriate plus or minus balance on current account.

10 General Survey

The centrepiece of this attempt to formulate some axioms that would be basic in a general theory of economic dynamics consists of the group of three eqations as follows:

$$G = \frac{s}{C}; \; G_w = \frac{s_d}{C_r}; \; G_n = \frac{s_a}{C_r} \; (\text{or } s_a = G_n C_r).$$

The G_w equation specifies what rate of growth is needed to enable saving as preferred to be equal to investment requirements. Saving is, of course, always and necessarily equal to investment; that fact is set out in the G equation. But the saving as currently accruing in fact may be above or below what people (including companies) had intended and now desire to make. The G_w equation shows the growth rate that is consistent with saving being equal to what people want it to be. Similarly the C_r in the G_w ('warranted' growth) equation represents the amount of additions to fixed capital and inventories that strikes suppliers as about right in relation to current or projected put-through. In growth some of them will continually be adding to their rate of ordering. But if the current accrual of real capital is equal to what they deem currently needed, they will not be modifying their rate of ordering upwards or downwards with a view to getting their real capital, fixed and circulating, into line with what they need. In fine, the 'warranted' growth rate is that which equates desired saving to the required increase of real capital.

Then there is quite a different growth rate, that I have called the 'natural' growth rate (G_n), namely the growth rate that fully utilises the increase in working population and also embodies technological progress as regards methods for providing goods and services, as and when it is available to be thus embodied. What is not widely recognised in current writing is that there are two normative growth rates, and that the one that enables investment requirements to absorb the savings that people want to make, and the one that corresponds to the increase of manpower and technological progress, currently becoming available for application, may be *entirely different*. Indeed it would be a mighty coincidence if these two growth rates, namely the one that suffices to embody proferred savings into real capital and the one that suffices to embody reasonably available technological progress were the same. I do not find this all important difference much stressed in current writing. It is clearly very fundamental to a correct theory of economic growth.

Presumably the authorities responsible for economic policy will, to the extent that they have a policy designed to influence the current level of activity in the economy, choose the achievement of the natural growth rate as their target. Let the economy achieve the maximum growth that its accretion of manpower and of the findings of applied science are capable of achieving.

A digression is in place here. 'Growth economists' have been criticised for giving priority to the increases of the goods and services that are included in the statistical measurement of national income, or of the 'G.D.P.' It is implied that they want to push on at all costs with the increase of the G.D.P., often at the sacrifice of other amenities that give pleasure to mankind, but are not included in the G.D.P. There are international league tables setting out the growth rates of the G.D.P.s in various countries and it is considered rather bad to be low down on the table. I, for my own part, wish to repudiate this attitude very emphatically. The U.K. has been low in the league tables in recent years; but I have the impression that the welfare of the average man has been rising more rapidly in the U.K. than in the other major countries.

An increase of leisure may be deemed to involve an increase of happiness, although it may cause, in the modern world – the matter was rather different in the early days of the Industrial Revolution and the Factory Acts – the growth of the G.D.P. to be less than it otherwise would be. I have some doubts about a further decrease in the length of the working day, since work should be a pleasure – see below. But an increase of holidays surely increases happiness.

Then there is the whole question of working conditions. An

improvement of these is surely likely to add to human happiness, even if it decreases the G.D.P., although it may not always do so. We have recently had a fine biography by Mrs Cole of her husband, Douglas Cole, who was the founder of what long ago was called Guild Socialism. Its main idea was that the workers should be masters of their fate and have legal power to regulate their own conditions of work, rather than be bossed in this respect by capitalist employers on the one hand or by a central socialist government on the other. Cole continued to take a deep interest in this throughout his life, long after the movement called Guild Socialism had faded from view. The greater achievement of self-government in workplaces might well add to human happiness, although it reduced the value of the G.D.P. as statistically calculated.

Then there is the question of preserving the amenities of the countryside and controlling the manner in which towns are developed. This is a sphere for government intervention, both positive and negative. Its positive interventions, e.g. by the provision of public parks, may well be underestimated – partly because they are valued at cost without profit – in the computations of the G.D.P. More important, restrictions, e.g. on how and where and what private enterprise is allowed to erect in or near towns, will by increasing happiness add to welfare and yet not contribute anything to the computed G.D.P. and may well reduce it by preventing or obstructing many money-making projects.

In this connection it should be added that the personnel engaged to implement such restrictions should be of the very best brain power, foresight and imagination. If there is a central government department addressed to this, it should be regarded as much more prestigious to have a place in it, than, say, in the Treasury or Foreign Office. The work in question will presumably have to be divided between the central and local authorities. In regard to the latter there may be a problem, since some places – not all – may lack local personnel of the right quality.

It is to be hoped that the foregoing has sufficed to safeguard the reader against the idea that growth economists wish an increase of G.D.P. to be given top priority, or priority over other amenities. What they do insist on, however, is that, subject to the foregoing limitations, economic growth should not be held down below the level otherwise achievable, for such purposes as checking domestic price inflation or rectifying the external balance of payments. Subject to the provision of amenities, subject to sufficient leisure, we want people to produce as many goods and services as the most up-to-date technology enables them to do. We do not want their work or output or employment to be curtailed, in order to cope with price inflation or an external imbalance. Other methods must be found for dealing with those problems.

In the formulation of the warranted growth rate (G_w), the term s_d appears, which stands for the amount that people currently wish to save expressed as a fraction income. 'People' consist of persons, of companies, and of governments, to the extent that the last mentioned think it prudent to save as part of their normal regime, whether to repay some debt or finance some reasonable proportion of their capital outlay. Savings (or dis-savings) made by a central government with the deliberate intention of regulating the economy, viz. preventing demand inflation or deflation, must be subtracted (dis-saving added), in assessing what the Government desires on its own account to save (governmental component of overall s_d).

It is to be stressed that defining s_d in this manner does *not* imply that people always, or even, usually, desire to save a constant fraction of their incomes. One might think it convenient to express the amount spent on cars in an economy as a fraction of its income rather than as so many pounds and pence; using such a notation would not carry the implication that people do in fact spend a constant fraction of their incomes through time on cars. The curve of expenditure on cars, based on this notation, might well be rising, falling or oscillating, according to the circumstances of the case; similarly with the amount that people desire to save, expressed as a fraction of income.

One might think it reasonable to believe that the size of income is usually the most important single determinant of the amount that people desire to save; but this may not be so in all cases; there may be other important determinants. There is all the difference in the world between expressing the amount that people desire to save as a fraction of income and affirming that they desire to save a constant fraction of income. The basic growth equations are rigid and precise, and it would be a 'howler' to introduce into them a sloppy generalisation about what determines the desires of people to save.

If the amount that people desire to save, expressed as a fraction of their incomes, is rising, then, with a constant C_r, the warranted growth rate will be rising also; and conversely. Such a rise cannot continue indefinitely unless there is a matching increase in the natural growth rate.

A rising C_r is conjugated with a falling warranted growth rate, and conversely. C_r will be constant if (i) technological progress is neutral (cf. Chapter 4) and (ii) the average capital intensity, in accordance with current technology, of the package of goods and services, on which citizens spend their successive increments of income, remains the same, or if there are changes under (i) and (ii) that exactly offset each other. Labour-saving technological progress entails a rising C_r (which entails a falling G_w) as does a trend in incremental consumption towards a more capital requiring package of goods and service S, given current technology.

Among various possible methods of producing a good or service, the one is chosen that shows the lowest cost, given the current prices of inputs, subject to the condition that the extra capital required for it, compared with the capital required for the method next below it on a list in which methods are listed in descending order of capital intensity, gets sufficient return. This 'condition' is important. It is possible that, on a list from A downwards of methods of descending capital intensity, method A has a lower cost, in terms of all inputs, including capital, than B, while at the same time the return on the extra capital required for method A is below the acceptable rate of return on capital and below the return on the extra capital required for method B, as compared with C. If the return on the capital required for method A is below what I have called the minimum acceptable rate of return on capital (MARC), it will not be adopted. This MARC is loosely related to the market rate of interest, but usually only after a considerable time-lag. And so we come around to the classic question of the influence of the rate of interest on the capital intensity of methods. I have expressed the opinion – but this is purely personal and must *not* be taken to be part of my economic dynamic theory – that the rate of interest and the MARC do not often have a big effect on the method chosen, since there are much more important influences governing the relative total costs of the various available methods. It may be allowed that a rise of the rate of interest to a substantially higher level, with interest continuing at around the new level, for years, rather than months, and expected to continue at that level within the relevant time-horizon, may have a substantial effect. Pure theory cannot tell us whether a rise of interest will tend to encourage or discourage saving. All depends on the elasticity of demand of savers for future income at the sacrifice of present income.

A lower capital intensity of productive methods is conjugated with a higher warranted growth rate, and conversely; and so is a higher saving ratio. Thus, unless the possible perverse effect of high interest in discouraging saving overtops its other effects, we may lay down that a higher interest rate entails, *pro tanto*, a higher warranted growth rate.

In the equation for the natural (optimum) growth rate, the optimum rate of interest, r, better the optimum MARC, is determined exclusively by the elasticity of the social diminishing utility of income curve. It has no connection with what individuals desire to save. It is to be noted in passing that the concept of MARC is just as applicable in the case of government enterprises as in that of private enterprise; indeed an equal MARC ought to be applied in both cases; otherwise there will be distortions in the use of productive resources.

There are difficulties in framing the concept of a rate of interest that should be included in the basic equations relating to warranted growth. It may presumably be taken for granted that, in the minds of most living economists, the old-time classical theory that the equilibrium market rate of interest was one that served to equate the supply of saving to the demand for investment purposes was killed stone dead by Keynes. There are as many such rates, he argued, as there are levels of employment, and there is nothing in market forces to ensure that they cause the actual rate to move to such a level (called by Keynes the 'neutral' rate) as will balance the supply of saving with the demand for capital disposal for investment at full employment. Such an outcome could only be by sublime coincidence. If the actual rate is to settle at the 'neutral' level, this will have to be by the deliberate management of the authorities. That relates to the macrostatic equilibrium.

The analogous problems become more intense when we go over to dynamics. There are various possible growth rates, each requiring it own different quantity of Saving (= Investment). Might someone be inclined to borrow from Keynes and postulate a dynamic 'neutral' rate of interest as the one which brought the warranted growth rate into equality with the natural growth rate. This really makes no sense. One may imagine desired saving as consisting of 10 per cent of income, with the warranted growth rate determined accordingly, while the natural rate would require a saving ratio of 15 per cent. Is it credible that monkeying with the interest rate could elicit all this extra saving? Or would the high rate be intended to crush down the capital intensity of methods of production; this could happen with astronomical interest rates. But the resulting state of affairs would not be a condition of growth at its natural rate.

The capital intensity of methods of production to be conjugated with a 'natural' growth rate should be determined by an interest rate, or, better, by a MARC, which reflects the diminishing utility of income through time. That is something entirely different from the aforementioned balancing feat.

The same arguments would apply in reverse in a high saving situation, in which it would not seem credible to suppose that low interest would reduce in great measure the desired saving ratios.

If the warranted rate is continuingly unequal to the natural rate, fiscal policy seems to be the obvious remedy. If private saving is inadequate to sustain growth at its natural rate, the Government can supplement it by Budget surpluses. And conversely: if there is oversaving, leading to stagnation and recurrent recessions, owing to insufficient aggregate demand, the Government can increase that demand by running Budget deficits. These remedies seem very simple, but are none the worse for that.

The British authorities have recently been running into a technical difficulty of a rather serious character. What follows must not be taken to imply they have based themselves on sound advice as regards the overall dynamic forces; they have probably been overprone to deflation. But, even if they had not been, the dilemma confronting them would have been very real.

On the one side, after 1945 the British Parliament decided to nationalise large sections of industry, and these were notably capital-requiring. There have recently been murmurs in certain quarters of further nationalisation, but it may be that these do not have to be taken too seriously. Incidentally the dilemma in question, which is actually the most serious confronting economic policymaking in the U.K., does not seem to be widely appreciated. There are seldom references to it by politicians, even by those opposed to nationalisation on principle, or by journalists or other popular writers.

The industries in question have large annual capital requirements. In the early days some of these were allowed to issue their own bonds, but, as these carried fixed interest and had Government guarantees, they were very similar to ordinary Government stock. Later the Government took over the job of providing the capital disposal that they needed. This it could do by issuing Government bonds to the public, or, in part, by having a surplus in the Budget of tax receipts over current expenditure. In the most recent period the Government has relied almost exclusively on the latter method.

For a number of years now investors have shown a diminishing appetite for Government bonds. In the middle sixties the yield of good equity shares fell below that on Government bonds for the first time in history. The main reason is probably that the range of large companies, well known to be of good long-term reliability, has increased considerably. Another reason, which has been more heavily stressed, and in the recent period probably correctly so, is that the shares of companies, unlike Government bonds, have a hedge against price inflation, and that the idea that price inflation will continue (hopefully not at its present (1971) rate), has become a widely accepted belief.

And so we have the dilemma, a need for the Government to provide capital year by year on a scale unparallelled in any non-socialist country, and a growing distaste on the side of investors for Government bonds. On top of this must be mentioned the large size of our National Debt, as inherited from two world wars, of which sizeable blocks come up every year for redemption, and the consequent need to sell replacement stocks in the market. This gives a headache to those who have to manage the National Debt. I am convinced that this day-by-day problem for the authorities has caused the Government to budget for a far larger Budget surplus than they would have done, if they had regulated their fiscal policy, i.e. the size of their Budget surplus, with a view to maintaining the growth of aggregate demand in the economy at its 'natural' rate. The large Budget surplus is a measure of very severe fiscal deflation, and this may well be the most important reason why the U.K. has in recent years been so low on the league table of national growth rates. This low place has little to do with alleged business inefficiency or troubles with the trade unions.

One way of meeting this difficulty would be to return to the old system of having the nationalised industry boards issue their own securities, while at the same time allowing them to introduce an equity element into their terms. In the early days this would have been frowned upon, as it would have seemed to be retaining the feature of the 'capitalist' system constituted by profit, which it was one of the main objectives of socialism and of nationalisation to eliminate. Ideas have become less rigid since then, and, when it comes to the investment of funds, socialists have no hesitation in recommending equities.

Of course the profit margin that the Boards would, under such a proposal, be allowed to add to costs would be subject to regulation based on agreed principles. It would not do to have them take advantage of their monopolistic position and take in monopolistic profit. When subject to this limitation, would their equities be able to compete, in the minds of the investors, with those of private enterprise? Investors in the latter may hope to participate in additional monopoly profit liable to accrue to private enterprise firms over the course of time. As against this limitation, the Boards would have the advantage of the permanent support of the Government. One might have a scheme by which if they ran into a period when they made a loss – as some have already done! – the Government would provide subsidies to enable dividends to be maintained. That would cost the taxpayers far less than the present system, whereby they not only have to provide current subsidies for nationalised industries, but also – a much greater burden – to provide out of their taxes the large amounts of fresh capital needed by the industries year by year. Those at present making losses would presumably not be included in the scheme.

One sometimes wonders about the pricing policies of some of the authorities. Railway fares go up and up. Might it not be better business to attract custom by reducing fares, not necessarily across the board, but for the types of journey where the road is in active competition? Not many years ago one calculated that, if one was travelling alone, it cost about the same to travel between London and Norfolk by car as by train. Now the train is very much more expensive. There must be millions of occasions when a traveller chooses the car, although the train would be more convenient, simply in order to economise. And what about the amenities of country and town, referred to at the outset of this chapter? Car travel is much more destructive of them than train travel.

In regard to government stock I made a cognate proposal some years ago. Why not make it more attractive by introducing flexible interest? It would be entirely contrary to public policy to introduce anything like a hedge against price inflation. That would be to admit defeat. It should be the firm stance of the authorities that they were absolutely determined to battle on manfully until price inflation was eliminated. But might one not issue a stock, the interest on which rose in proportion to the increase in national productivity? This must not of course be the increase postulated by some planner, but the increase as recorded year by year in the statistics.

In regard to the target of maintaining aggregate demand at its correct level, monetary policy may be brought in to aid fiscal policy. The trouble about this is that monetary policy has so many jobs to do. If fiscal policy can achieve this particular task without assistance, and there is no clear reason why it should not be able to, subject to the aforementioned difficulties of debt management, it would seem prudent to leave the hands of the monetary authorities free to achieve their other tasks.

Inequality between the warranted and natural growth rates (oversaving and undersaving) is likely to be a continuing phenomenon. There may be a tendency towards convergence or divergence. There may of course from time to time be humps or dips in the curves representing the successive values of the rates through time, especially in the warranted rate, as affected by capital requirements (C_r) owing to some new invention (e.g. nuclear energy) requiring a large amount of capital outlay that has a significant value relatively to the economy as a whole. But the capital developments consequent on the invention are likely to take a number of years to reach their maximum, so that a consequent dip in the G_w curve is likely to be flattened out. There may be a consequent hump in the natural growth rate curve, but this will come after the dip in the warranted growth curve caused by the event in question. On the whole the convergence (or divergence) of the natural growth rate and the warranted rate, when unregulated, is likely to be a slow-moving process. Accordingly, the regulatory weapon designed to bring them together, as near as maybe, will often need to be kept in operation for considerable periods of time. This seems appropriate for fiscal policy. A government can continue to run Budget surpluses (or deficits) as a matter of regular policy year after year. Indeed, if the fiscal weapon can be given a long range task and if quick reversals of the engine are not expected of it, that simplifies life for all.

Policy advisers and relevant Ministers are apt to complain that it takes so long to get legislatures to implement what they ask for. Particularly in the U.S.A. it is complained that it often takes several years to get Congress to alter course in the direction recommended by the Administration, and that, by that time, what is done may be too late. Complaints of the non-compliance of the legislature are also heard in Germany. In Britain the case is somewhat different, since Parliament is normally under the control of the Cabinet. These complaints of 'too late' imply that it should be possible to rely on fiscal policy, to deal with quick-moving changes. This misconceives what should be the proper main objective of fiscal policy – the bringing together of the warranted and the natural growth rates, viz. the correction of the tendency of an unregulated economy to save too little or too much.

Monetary policy can be brought into action quickly, when the authorities decide that there is need for action. The central bank can put its foot on the accelerator or the brake right away. In regard to the objective of the equating the warranted to the natural rate, it might be called in aid occasionally. For instance, it might come in useful on the occasions of the humps or dips in the warranted rate as already described. But on the whole monetary policy should be reserved for its other very important tasks.

The foregoing has been concerned with the possible and indeed highly probable inequality of the natural growth rate and the (unregulated) warranted growth rate. Next to be considered are the runaways of the actual growth rate from the warranted rate. Just as it would be a remarkable coincidence if the warranted rate were equal to the natural, so also it would be a coincidence if at a point of time the actual rate was equal to the warranted rate. There is, however, this difference. Whereas the divergence of the unregulated warranted rate is apt to be fairly stable for substantial periods and to change rather slowly, a divergence of the actual rate from the warranted increases rapidly in the short period. Accordingly, the quick-acting weapon of monetary policy is suitable, and indeed necessary, to correct the latter divergence.

The main objective of monetary policy so far as the home front is concerned, is to prevent demand-pull inflation on the one hand and increasing underemployment on the other. Both tendencies, if uncorrected, may gather momentum rapidly. It would be foolish to hope that fiscal weapons could be brought into play sufficiently quickly to check these movements unaided; furthermore the use of fiscal policy for such a task might undermine its efficiency in achieving its long-range objective. Nonetheless there may be certain occasions when it may be a lesser evil to use it, if there has been previous monetary mismanagement. The nature of the runaway movements was described in Chapter 3 and further discussed in Chapter 7.

Against a background of responsible fiscal policy, monetary policy should always be able to check a demand-pull inflation. By 'responsible' policy it is meant that the Government is not running large deficits in excess of any 'over-saving' that there may be by persons and companies. The exigencies of war time may make it needful to run such deficits. In that case there is nothing that the monetary authorities can do to prevent demand-pull inflation. (Do the 'monetarists' have a contrary opinion?) If price inflation is to be checked in such circumstances direct controls are necessary.

Doubt has been expressed about the importance, and even direction, of the quantitative effect of interest rate changes on the saving ratio, and about the quick effect of such changes on the capital output ratio, both because the MARC is sluggish in relation to interest changes and because the reaction of the capital output ratio to changes in the MARC may often not be quantitatively very important. It does not follow that monetary policy cannot have important effects. I have retained the opinion over a very long period that monetary policy has effects of crucial significance.

Interest rate changes are correlated with changes in the money supply. There is not always an exact correlation in the fairly short term. Attempts have been made to have a dual policy of lowering (or raising) long-term rates while raising (or lowering) short-term interest rates, usually in order to restrain the external outflow of capital while maintaining easy money at home, so as not to depress domestic activity; or conversely. Such dual policies operating by different rates of central bank sales or, perhaps, purchases of short- and long-term securities respectively appear to have had some success, but only for quite short periods. The link between the spectrum of interest rates and the money supply has remained.

The principal way in which a restrictive money supply policy serves to reduce the level, or rate of growth, of aggregate demand, is not by its effect in raising market interest rates, but by making it more difficult for firms that desire to expand operations to borrow. The capital market that confronts firms that seek to raise funds is an imperfect one. The firms have their traditional contacts, and they may seek out new contacts, if the former fail them. There are the clearing banks, other banks, the importance of which has recently increased, and other financial institutions and syndicates supplying finance for business. If all these are, across the board, rendered short of reserves by the monetary policy of the central bank, they will have to refuse to grant accommodation that in easier monetary conditions they would have been readily willing to grant. Enterprises, looking around, find that they just cannot raise, through one channel or another, the capital disposal that they need to finance real capital formation that they think likely to be profitable. The current British proposal that the non-clearing banks should be subjected to 'reserve requirements' may possibly make monetary deflation more prompt and efficient.

The consequence of the shortage of obtainable accommodation through the various available channels is a reduction of orders by businesses below the level at which they would otherwise have stood. The monetary authorities can carry a tight money policy to the point at which the aggregate of orders no longer exceeds the supply potential of the economy; in other words they can bring demand-pull inflation to an end. They normally have a complete power to eliminate demand-pull inflation.

Price inflation due to wage-price spiralling is an entirely different matter. Monetary and fiscal policies together have no power to prevent it, but might possibly on certain occasions have some influence on it. This matter may be elucidated with precision. Excessive aggregate demand entails that prices shall rise by more than money costs. When prices and wages are chasing each other, demand-pull inflation necessarily means that prices must rise more than costs. This may give an independent impetus to the wage-price chase itself. It may add fuel to the flames. If this influence on the aggregate demand factor in raising prices can be eliminated, this may reduce the fury of the chase between wages and prices. This is not certain, and cannot be presented as an axiom of economic dynamics, but it has some plausibility. On the other side of the blanket, it is probable that depressing aggregate demand substantially *below* the supply potential of the economy tends to increase the pace of any wage-price spiralling that may be proceeding. Depressing aggregate demand below the supply potential is likely to raise unit costs of production and thereby raises the fraction of wage increases that firms have to put into increased prices. That will accelerate the wage-price spiralling. The holding down of the rate of expansion by excessively restrictive monetary policies in the U.S.A. and Britain in recent years may actually have been a cause of the acceleration of the wage-price spiralling in those two countries in the 1969–71 period. But of course it was not the sole cause. For the main cause we have to look to *sociological* factors. In this case direct interference, whether on a voluntary or mandatory basis, will be needed, if the spiralling is to be terminated.

When it is a question of raising aggregate real demand, the potency of monetary policy is not so sure. The money supply may may increase sufficiently to provide the various agencies that normally lend to business with enough liquidity to agree to all propositions that seem reasonably sound. Any restraint that there may previously have been, owing to the agencies having insufficient reserves to meet all requests that are reasonable in themselves, comes to an end. Entrepreneurs cease to be held back from projects because those normally making funds available to them refuse to do so.

Nevertheless, easy money in this sense may not in all circumstances suffice to cause an expansion of activity and employment of appreciable amount. This could happen if, owing to a severe recession continuing to date, the great majority of entrepreneurs find themselves with capital equipment on hand that is substantially redundant to their current needs. They will say: 'We want to see an actual expansion in the demand for what we produce before adding still further to our redundant capacity.' A similar argument will apply in the case of inventories. But an increase in the money supply does not in and by itself increase demand. If there is no present increase in demand coming in to them, the purveyors of goods and services will have no motive for increasing their orders. Only if an appreciable number of entrepreneurs have been previously held by lack of finance from placing orders, that *in existing circumstances* they have been wanting to place, will easy money by itself cause an increase of orders. That will set the ball rolling. The Multiplier Effect of those additional orders will cause a general diffusion of increased activity through the economy. But if, in the immediately antecedent period, only a negligible minority had been restrained from placing orders for additions to capital owing to the difficulty of obtaining the needed finance, easy money will not set the ball rolling.

I attach no importance to what is called the 'Pigou effect'; indeed I believe that this theory is based on an underlying fallacy. It is argued that consumers, finding that the part of the increased money supply, as provided by the authority, that comes into their hands is redundant to their needs, will spend it on consumption. But their total capital, including therein their cash holding, will not have increased. Their increased money will be at the expense of a diminished holding of securities. If they use their extra money to buy consumer goods they will be 'living on capital'. Well, many people are living on capital all the time; but their actions in this respect are more than offset by the greater weight of people who spend less than their incomes. There is no reason why the inception of easier money should cause persons suddenly to decide to live beyond their means, when they were not doing so before. Rather, what they will seek to do will be to restore the previous relation of their securities to their cash holding. The change in the composition of their assets will not have been intentional. It will have come to them by accident, so to speak, at the end of the day. They will plan to restore the previous ratio of securities to cash, and the great majority will actually restore it.

But they cannot all do so, because the 'easier money policy' will have been effectuated by a swap, first by the central bank, and then quickly followed by the deposit banks, of securities for cash with the non-bank public. There will, by consequence, be available to the non-bank public a smaller amount of securities and a larger amount of money. This non-bank public will seek to restore its ratio of securities to cash by buying the former. This will tend to raise the prices of securities and thereby reduce their current yield. The great majority of persons will invest despite this. But, as the prices of securities rise, there will be a fringe, mainly at the business end of the non-bank public, which will be deterred from purchasing securities by the decline in their yield. They will argue to themselves that, if they wait a little, the yield on securities will presently rise. And they will usually be right, since, when an easy money policy is effective in causing a revival, interest rates or 'yields' tend to go up very soon after such revival.

This is the basic Keynesian doctrine of 'liquidity preference'; and it is incompatible with the 'Pigou effect' doctrine. The former has, in my opinion, superior logical force; and it was propounded by a man who had a far greater understanding of the intermeshing of pure economic theory with the sequence of events than Pigou.

Accordingly, if a recession has been allowed to gather momentum and to last for a substantial period, monetary measures may be ineffective. The moral is that monetary measures ought to be adopted *promptly*. There is no technical difficulty in doing this. A central bank can start its purchase of securities on the day. The longer a recession or a stagnation has continued, the less effective will monetary policy be. Therefore, it is very important that an easy money policy should be adopted as soon as there are any symptoms of recession, or indeed, more strictly, as soon as there are any symptoms of the growth rate of orders falling below the growth rate of the supply potential of the economy. Some modification of this may be required if, as at present (November 1971) in Germany, there is a substantial backlog of unfulfilled orders. The existence of such a backlog is a symptom of previous mismanagement.

It is at the *top* of the boom that the monetary authorities should be most vigiliant for the right moment at which to increase the money supply. The longer they delay after that, the less effective will their measures be.

There are two major inequalities of growth rates in the normal course of things. One is the difference between the warranted growth rate, as determined by what people want to save, and the 'required' level of investment (the capital-output ratio), and the 'natural growth rate', as determined by the increase (or decrease) of the working population and by technological progress. The other is the inequality between the actual growth rate and the warranted growth rate. (1. $G_w \neq G_n$. 2. $G \neq G_w$)

The theme of the foregoing arguments is that fiscal policy should be primarily concerned with the first mentioned inequality ($G_w \neq G_n$); and that monetary policy should be primarily concerned with the second mentioned inequality ($G \neq G_w$). The former is susceptible to rather slow modification through time and the requirements for change in it will be slow-moving. The monetary weapon is capable of rapid changes and the requirement for its use for its purpose will come on rapidly. But we should think that monetary policy and fiscal policy should both be called in occasionally to help each other to fulfil their respective tasks, as specified. Neither, nor both together, can correct the great evil of wage-price spiralling; for this we need a third instrument of policy and, to date, the only one known to us is direct interference with wage bargains and price fixing ('incomes policy').

What about the external balance of payments? What instrument of policy should get this into equality? It has sometimes been postulated that appropriate domestic monetary and fiscal policies will automatically secure an equal external balance by consequence. This idea has no foundation in economic theory or in experience. There is no doubt that a domestic deflationary policy, carried to the extent of causing a decline of activity and increasing underemployment, can correct an adverse external balance by reducing import requirements. But there is a conflict here. Should we tolerate an increase of underemployment and a reduction of production with a view to restoring the external balance? Are not other weapons of policy available for that purpose? It is to be noted that, in consequence of the required reduction of activity, the decrease of output of goods and services entailed will be of far larger quantity than that of the external deficit that it is desired by this method to eliminate. Therefore a reduction of domestic activity in order to improve an external balance is a recipe that should be *outlawed* from the standpoint of aggregate world welfare, and, accordingly, from the standpoint of political economy.

What can be done to abate or eliminate wage-price spiralling is beneficial both to the domestic economy, and also to the external balance, provided that the elasticities of demand are right, as they may be presumed usually to be.

There is growing recognition that the idea of regularly using the weapon of reducing domestic output and employment is unsatisfactory, and even barbarous. This has caused thought to move to the idea of flexible exchange rates as a more acceptable method of restoring an external balance, when it is in deficit. The method in question divides into the idea that an adjustment of parities, as already allowed in the constitution of the International Monetary Fund, should be applied more frequently, and the idea of having no fixed parity ('floating' exchange rates). The objection to the infrequent use of the 'adjustable peg', as allowed by the constitution of the I.M.F., namely only after it has become plain that an adjustment (upward or downward) is appropriate, is that wise financial advisers will think ahead and activate a very large international movement of funds, in advance of the gravely considered decision of the authorities to alter the parity. The consequent international movements of funds have been of vast dimensions, as described in Chapter 9, and the very large mutual supports among central banks ('swap credits') arranged to offset these movements have not always been sufficient to prevent the movements making it necessary for countries to revalue, even when they have not thought revaluation appropriate.

It has been suggested that the 'adjustable peg', as allowed by the I.M.F. constitution should be used more frequently, so that there would not be time for a massive international movement of funds, anticipatory of an impending adjustment, to build up. This is probably correct. But there is the counter-view that, if it became a habit, and this was known, as it would have to be, that it was the policy to have more frequent changes of parity, the advisers to companies with international interests would take *smaller* events, likely to alter balances of payments, as reasons for advising their companies to shift funds. In that case the embarrassment due to such shifting, with it being established that there would be more frequent changes of exchange parities, might be no less than if it were assumed that the changes in question would be more rare. If this matter could be econometrically analysed, which is of course quite impossible at present, although it might be possible in the twenty-first century, it might be feasible to establish the optimum period between revaluations, on overall average, to minimise the pressures due to anticipatory movements between countries of the funds of multi-national companies.

There has recently been coming into favour, among economic theorists, although not among those involved in practical operations, the idea of having no fixed official parities; the operative exchange rates would be governed by market forces. This idea has its attractiveness. The objection to it is that the fluctuation of the exchange rate would be an obstacle to the optimum flow of international trade, owing to the uncertainty caused by it. It has been counter-argued that these uncertainties can be removed by operations in 'forward' foreign exchange operations. This is not so. At present the forward foreign exchange market does not provide cover for more than around six months. This period may in due course be extended, but the outsider cannot know how quickly. Meanwhile, there is no doubt that many decisions as regards trade depend on considerations extending over a much longer, and growing, period. In many cases actual contracts for the delivery of goods extend over a two- to three-year period. And plans about efforts to push trade or make investments abroad may have an even longer time horizon. These points of view are certainly adverse to the project of having indeterminate exchange rates.

The project for having 'floating' rates divides into that for having 'managed' floating rates or freely floating rates. Freely floating rates would cause large oscillations and consequently be especially adverse to the convenience of traders. Some 'management' of the rate not only would be highly desirable, in order to maintain international trade at a reasonable level, but also, in terms of practical realities, inevitable. The expression 'dirty floating' has recently been applied to managed floating in the confused period after 15 August 1971. This has related to official intentions designed to secure certain strategic objectives in relation to a prospective refixing of parities. This is quite different from those interventions ('management') that would be essential in a regime of floating rates, when there was no prospect or intention of re-establishing fixed rates.

The only major example in practical experience of a floating rate, apart from minor countries (like Canada) and countries plunging into excessive domestic inflation and external devaluation, like some countries in Latin America, is that of sterling vis-à-vis gold standard countries, of which the U.S.A. was much the most important, in the period from 1931 to 1939 (or perhaps 1936). The 'float' was heavily managed by the Bank of England; the U.S.A. pursued a policy of 'benign neglect' (to use a more recent expression), in fact. They did not actually refer to this, although they could have done it with less detriment to themselves in the thirties, as they had then a vast gold reserve, than in 1970. Thus the Bank of England in effect managed the floating rate, ironing out both oscillations that would have been due to seasonal factors and to the large temporary inflow and outflow of refugee capital from the other main countries.

In a multiple system of managed floating rates, daily consensuses would be required, and that would be technically difficult. It was represented to me recently that this presented no technical difficulty owing to the international telephone system; the various parties could settle with each other in the course of a few minutes what the mutual rates should be, so as to avoid irregular cross-rates. That is doubtless so at the purely technical level. But with management there are problems of policy at a high level. The British, for instance, may believe that a current pressure on sterling should be allowed to exert its influence, not being due to transient and reversible factors, while the Americans may at the same time believe the contrary, and consequently hold that letting sterling move downwards in the circumstances would be un-neighbourly and disruptive. And the French and Germans, etc., may have different views on this topic both in regard to sterling and their own rates against the dollar. Such matters cannot be decided by technical foreign exchange operators each morning; consensus is needed from personages of high level in the government hierarchy, who, every morning, find a great many papers of serious consequence on their desk. The idea that there would be no problem of obtaining consensus each morning among personages at that level in the various important countries is extremely remote from practical reality.

Even at the technical level the problem is not so simple. I recall a number of years ago someone well versed in these matters saying that, after a few weeks of floating rates, the exchange rate operators would communicate with each other, multi-laterally, saying 'for Heaven's sake let us agree at what rates to operate' and obtain joyful agreement. Thus the low-level operators would in effect establish *fixed* exchange rates for the time; there would then not be floating rates at all, but an adjustable peg system.

In relation to the flexible exchange rate remedy for an imbalance there is the deeper problem of the elasticities of supply and demand possibly being insufficient for a devaluation to cause an improvement or an upward valuation to reduce a surplus. Recent experience suggests that revaluations cannot always be relied on to change the balance of trade in the direction intended. Economists of distinction, like Professor J. E. Meade, have affirmed that, while a short-term change in an appropriate direction cannot be relied on, there is a probability of the long-run change being in the right direction. This is probably true. It implies, however, that, if policies depend on exchange rate changes under a flexible exchange rate system, it is needful for countries to have larger reserves to tide over the interval in which the exchange rate movement will not have its needed effect.

I am convinced that larger reserves are needed to operate a managed floating-rate system than are needed for a fixed-rate system. This was certainly the British experience in the period 1925–39. When Britain went over, in September 1931, from a fixed-rate to a managed floating-rate system, there was in fact a much larger use of reserves, and a need to use them, than there had been in the fixed-rate period. This is in direct contradiction to the view widely held, not only among ivory tower theorists, but in a wider circle. When there is anxious discussion about how to get world reserves to expand in accordance with need, they argue: 'Why not, instead, go over to floating rates and then this reserve problem will disappear?' The opposite is the case.

Those on an extremely high ivory tower, who request unmanaged floating rates, argue that no reserves would be needed, and this is theoretically correct. But they do not get support from those not on the Tower, who, correctly, argue that a system of non-managed floating rates is not a feasible system, owing to the vast impediments that it would place in front of a normal flow of international trade and investment.

Finally there is the question of whether we should regard international capital movement as the balancing item, when the current account, as influenced by the various forces operating on it, is out of balance; the sum of all forces operating on the current account may cause it to be growingly out of balance as time proceeds.

In my judgement there should be restrictions on (or, on occasion, special encouragements to) the international flow of capital, which should be related to an optimum. This matter is discussed in Chapter 9. The imbalance, growing or declining, in the current account is clearly relevant, but it should *not* be regarded as an *a priori* criterion for establishing the optimum international flow of capital, or for determining what interferences governments should initiate as regards the flow of international capital that is actually proceeding.

If the overall basic balance, consisting of the current balance under free trade and the optimum capital flow, is not equal, then some further interference will be necessary. It is the duty of each country to ensure an equal balance. It is not an acceptable view that a country, even if it is the most important in the world, like the U.S.A., should view this problem with 'benign neglect', and leave it to other countries to clear up the mess. Accordingly, if the sum of the current account items and optimum long-term capital movements do not yield an equal balance, some further interference will be needed, in addition to that required to secure an optimum capital movement.

It will then be an open question whether this additional interference should be with trade (or with other current account items) or with capital movement. There is no justification for the view that interference with capital should be preferred *a priori* to any interference with trade. This idea, which is widely prevalent, is an example of muddled thinking, alas, not untypical of still continuing thought about applied economics. If it is true that the optimum flow of trade can, hopefully, be secured with a minimum of interference, while the optimum flow of capital cannot usually be secured without substantial interference, it does *not* follow that, if interference is needed to secure an equal external balance, one should think in the first instance of interference with capital movement. 'International capital movement is something that one normally interferes with, and ought to; trade is not; therefore, if there is an overall basic imbalance, interfere with capital.' Could anything be more muddled-headed? The fact that, in order to get the optimum current account flow, less interference is usually needed than to get the optimum capital flow is no reason whatever for assuming that, if the combined effect of the two flows leads to an overall basic imbalance, there is a presumption in favour of interfering with the capital flow, rather than with the trade flow. The matter has to be considered on the merits of the case. If, unhappily, the combined effect of the optimum trade flow and the optimum capital flow is not to secure an equal balance, then some interference with one or other optimum is needed. No nation (like the U.S.A. in the 1957–71 period) should view an overall unequal balance with 'benign neglect'. The idea that the combined effect of the two imbalances will automatically secure an equal overall basic balance belongs to an obsolete economic theory.

Accordingly the problem is whether interference with trade (and other current account terms) or interference with capital, will have the less adverse effect on human welfare. If there is an imbalance of £x million, one has to estimate what amount of interference will be needed to rectify it, or, rather, in dynamics, one has to consider whether x is increasing or declining. If it is declining, then the moral is *not* to interfere with the optimum on current or capital account. This presupposes the availability of ample reserves of international media, to finance the deficits during the period, which obviously ought to be reckoned in terms of years, during which the unequal balance moves to an equal balance. But if the tendency of the two optima is in the other direction, namely to increase the imbalance, then the need for interference with the two optima (trade and capital flow) must be faced.

My own impression is that the loss of welfare due to loss of the marginal benefits of free international trade is likely to be *less* than the loss due to a deviation from the optimum capital flow. The trouble is that it is much more easy to establish the optimum level of international trade (roughly that of free trade) than it is to establish the optimum international capital flow. So, the prevailingly current maxim is that, if you have to interfere with either optimum, interfere with capital movement rather than with trade. Our estimate of probable loss due to a certain course of action depends on a probability spectrum. The most probable point on it has to be considered in conjunction with the spread of the umbrella (the spectrum of probabilities) on each side of it. If it is the case that the umbrella relating to the deviation of trade from its optimum is narrower than that covering capital movements, then there is a presumption that interference with trade, such as is needed to secure an improvement in the external balance of $£x$, is likely to do more harm than an interference with capital movements such as, on the best estimate, is likely to improve the basic balance by $£x$.

This assumes that the spectrum of probabilities in regard to interference with capital movements is a more widely spread umbrella than those relating to interference with trade. That may be so. It is to be hoped that research and planning will reduce the spread of the capital movements umbrella. But even if it is at present so, in relation to most cases, it does not follow that interference with capital movement should be taken to have an *a priori* justification as against interference with trade. Whatever the spread of the umbrella, the most likely loss, due to an interference with the optimal capital flow may be much greater than an interference with trade flow sufficient to have an equal quantitative effect. This issue can only be determined by empirical research. Economic theory provides no reason for holding that interference with the international capital flow is less detrimental to welfare than an interference with the trade flow producing an equal change in the international balance of payments. After the U.S.A. had got into difficulties with its external balance (1957), Presidents Kennedy and Johnson laid stress on reducing capital outflow; that may have been quite right in the circumstances. But later President Nixon's measures (15 August 1971) laid greater stress on reducing imports; this was followed by world-wide criticism, but it may well have been better from the point of view of world welfare than any further interference with the capital flow. It is true that from this point of view the outflow of U.S. capital (cf. Chapter 9) may be excessive; but no reasoning was supplied in relation to what corrective measures should have been taken in 1971 to redress the long continuing adverse U.S. balance.

I conclude by summarising what, on any view, should be the agenda for economists in the years immediately ahead. First and foremost, we need an agreed set of basic axioms for economic dynamics, up to the standard of those formulated by Alfred Marshall and Pareto in the field of micro-statics, and as subsequently modified by the theory of 'imperfect competition'. Secondly we need an agreed set of axioms, flowing therefrom, for the economic policies of the various countries. Their official statements of their reasons for initiating various measures are usually entirely out of line with modern economic dynamics. Thirdly, and finally, we need to establish methods for assessing the current trends of events that are related to dynamic theory and its practical applications. To date, the explanations of the reasons for policy presented by the highest authorities have seemed to be very inadequate.

I should not like to end on a pessimistic note. It is my opinion that economics, both theoretical and applied, and as understood by those responsible for policy has greatly advanced since 1945, and has contributed much to human welfare since that date.

Index